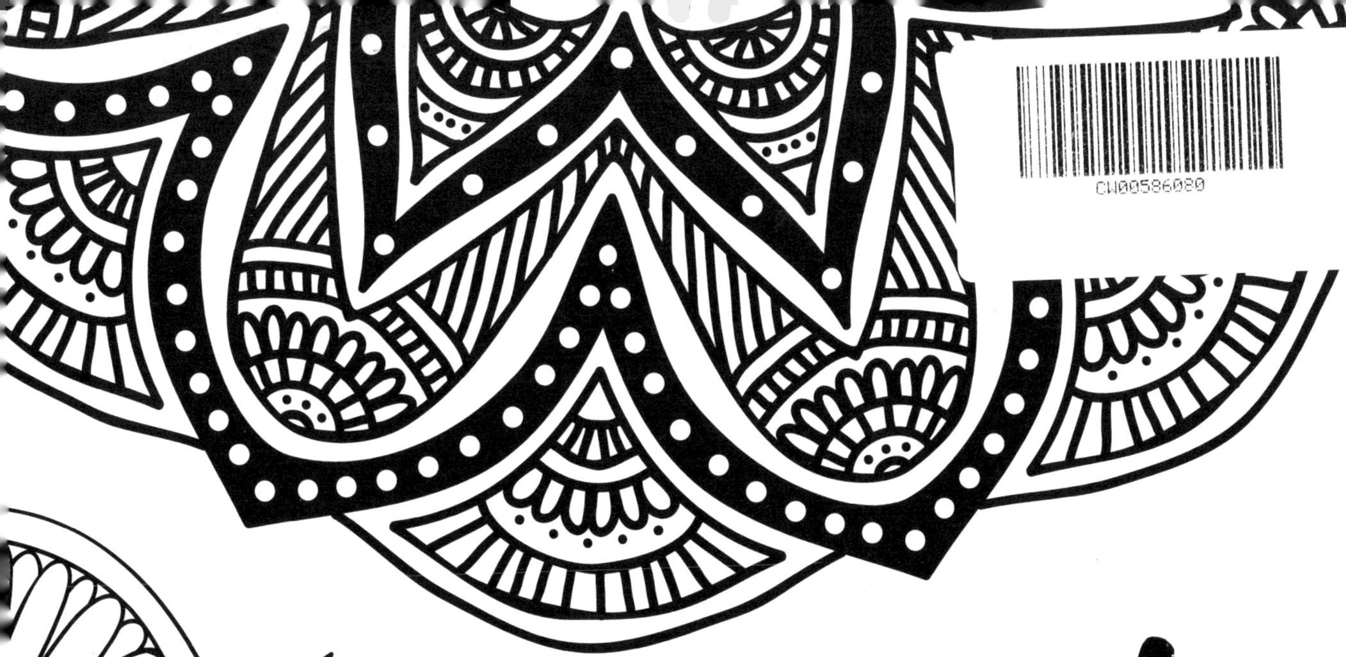

Art Therapy

COLOURING BOOK

Mandalas & More

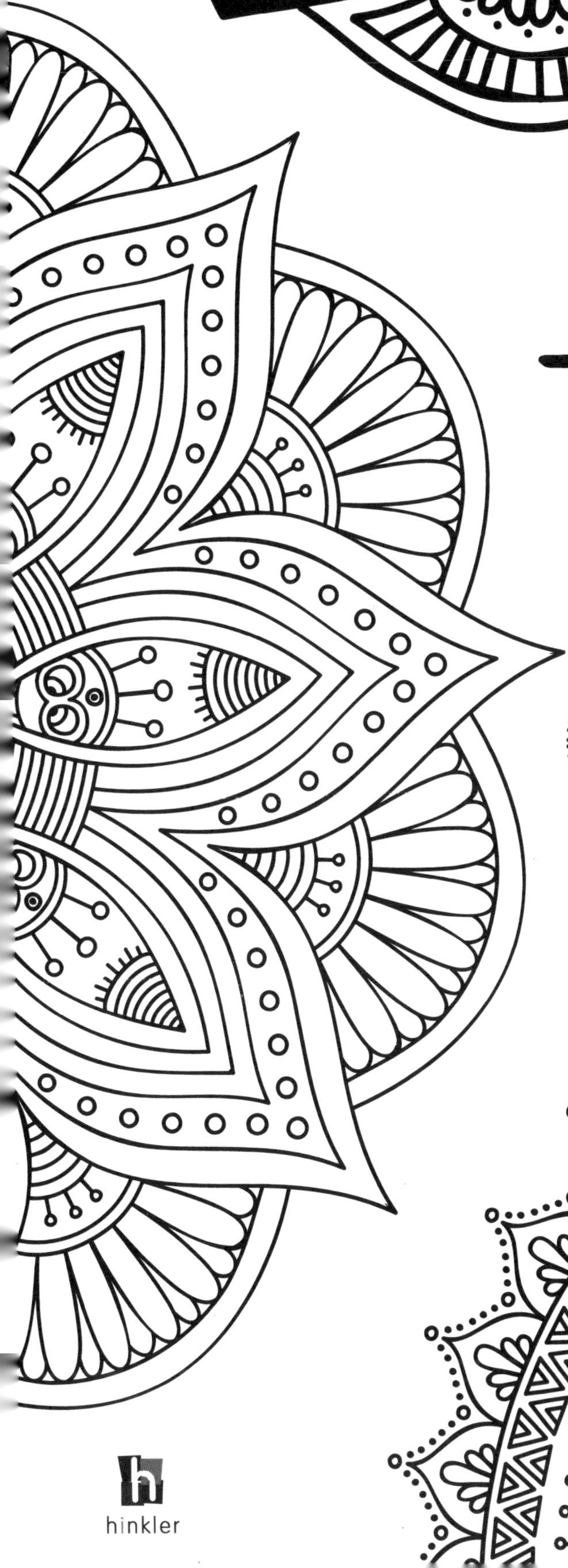

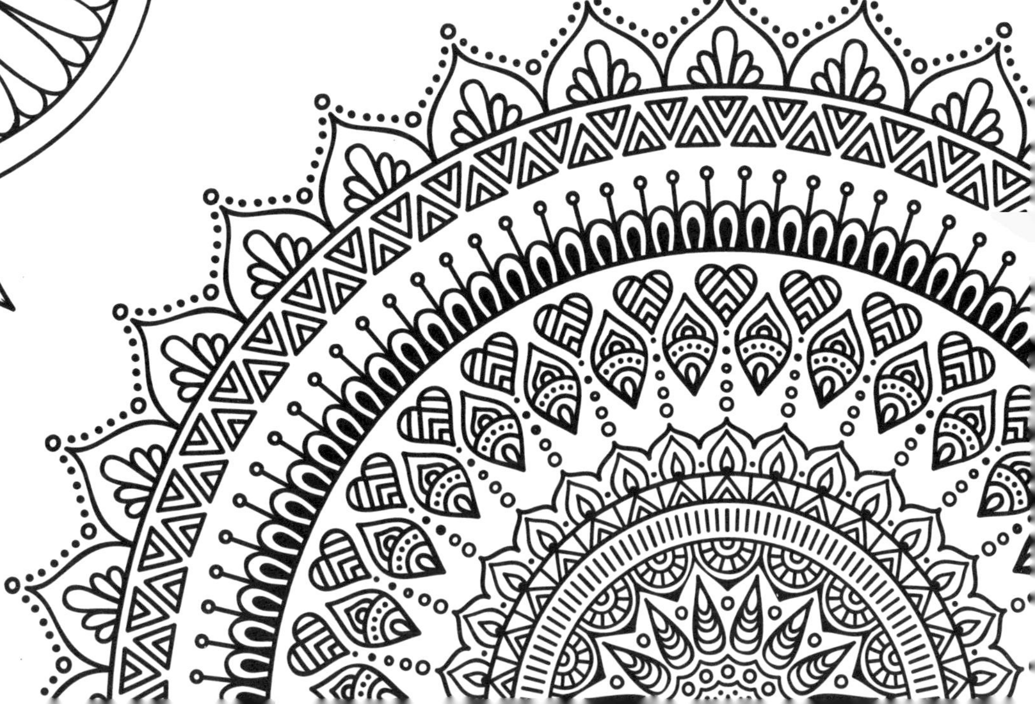

hinkler

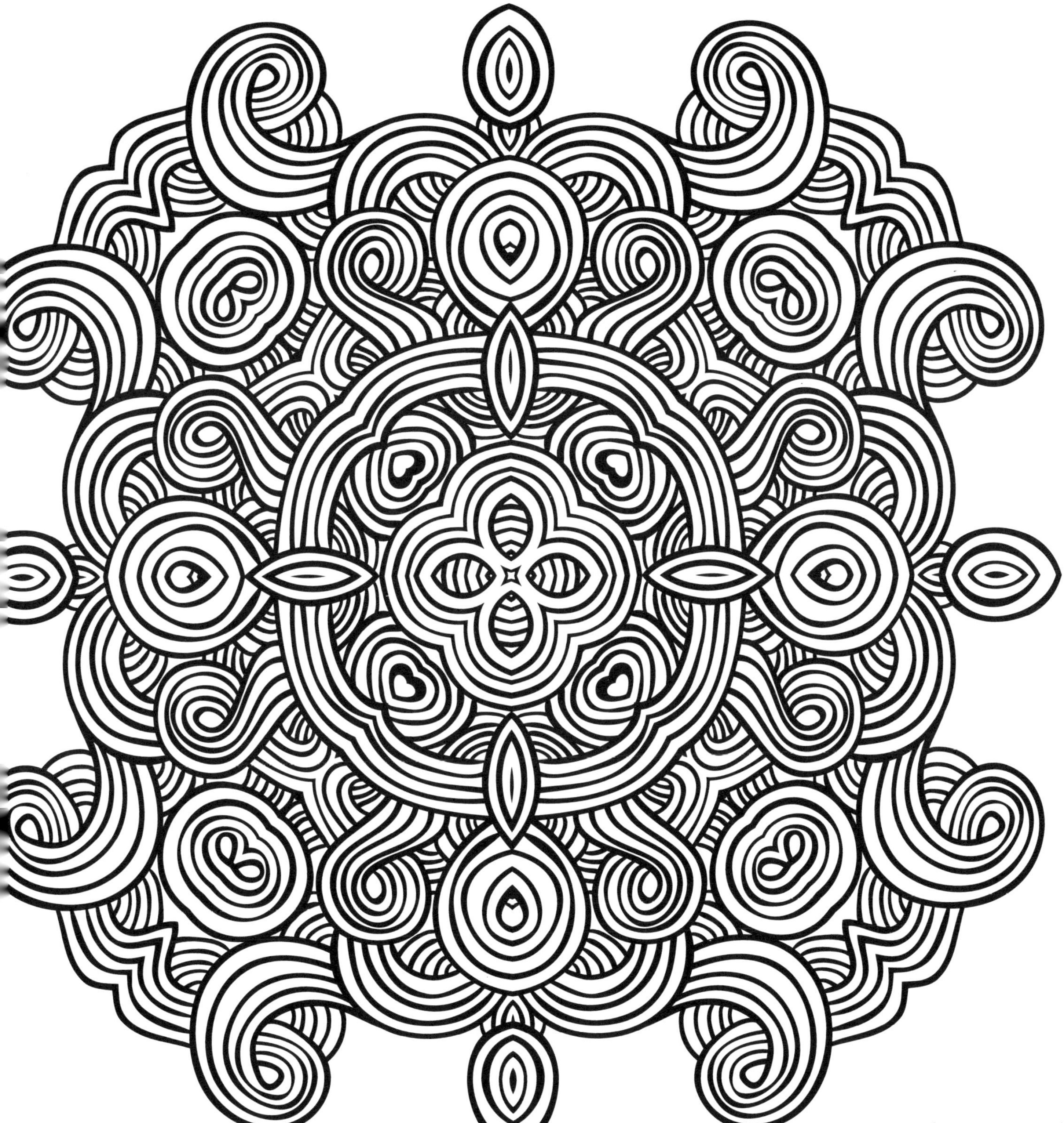

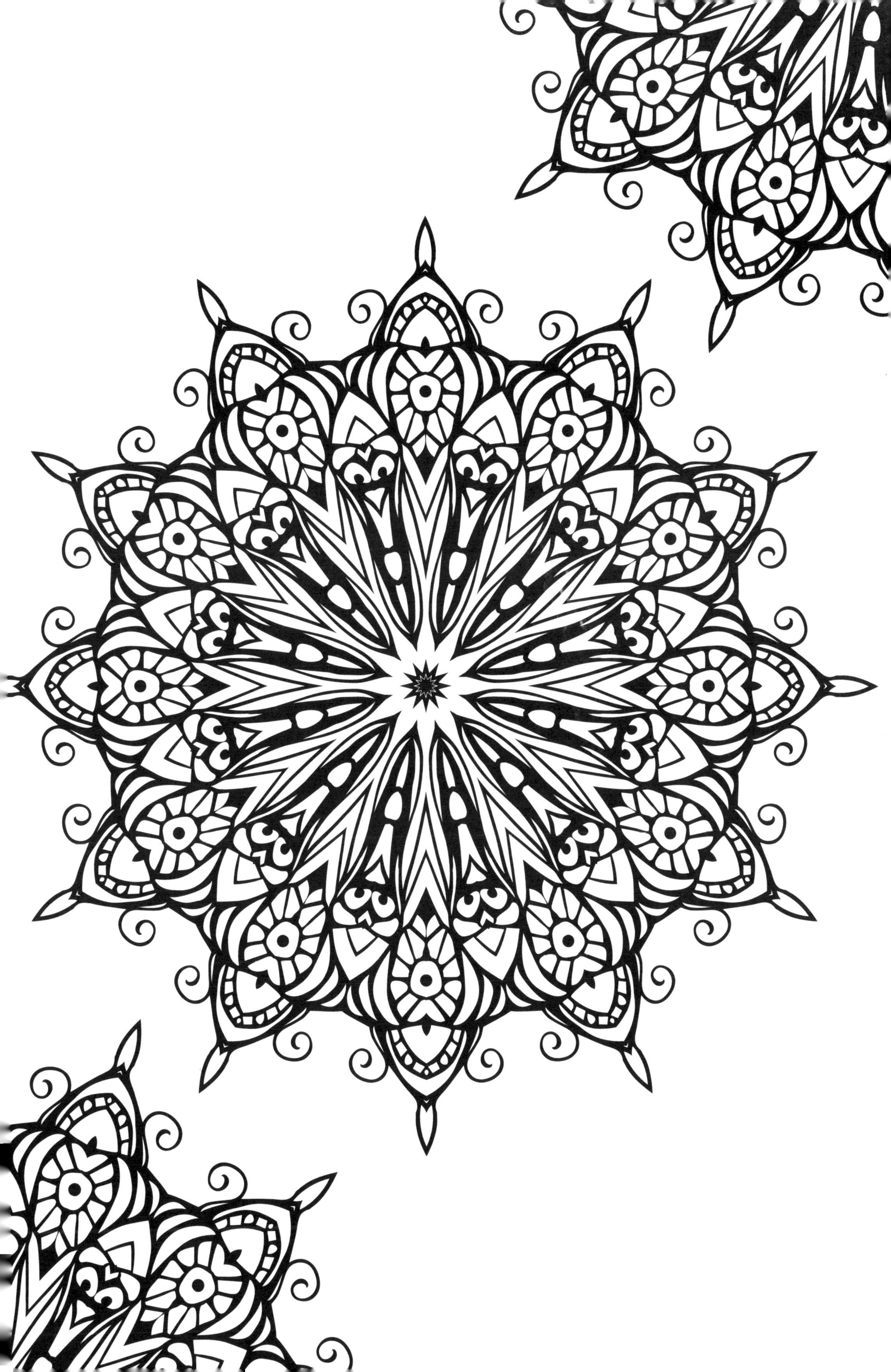

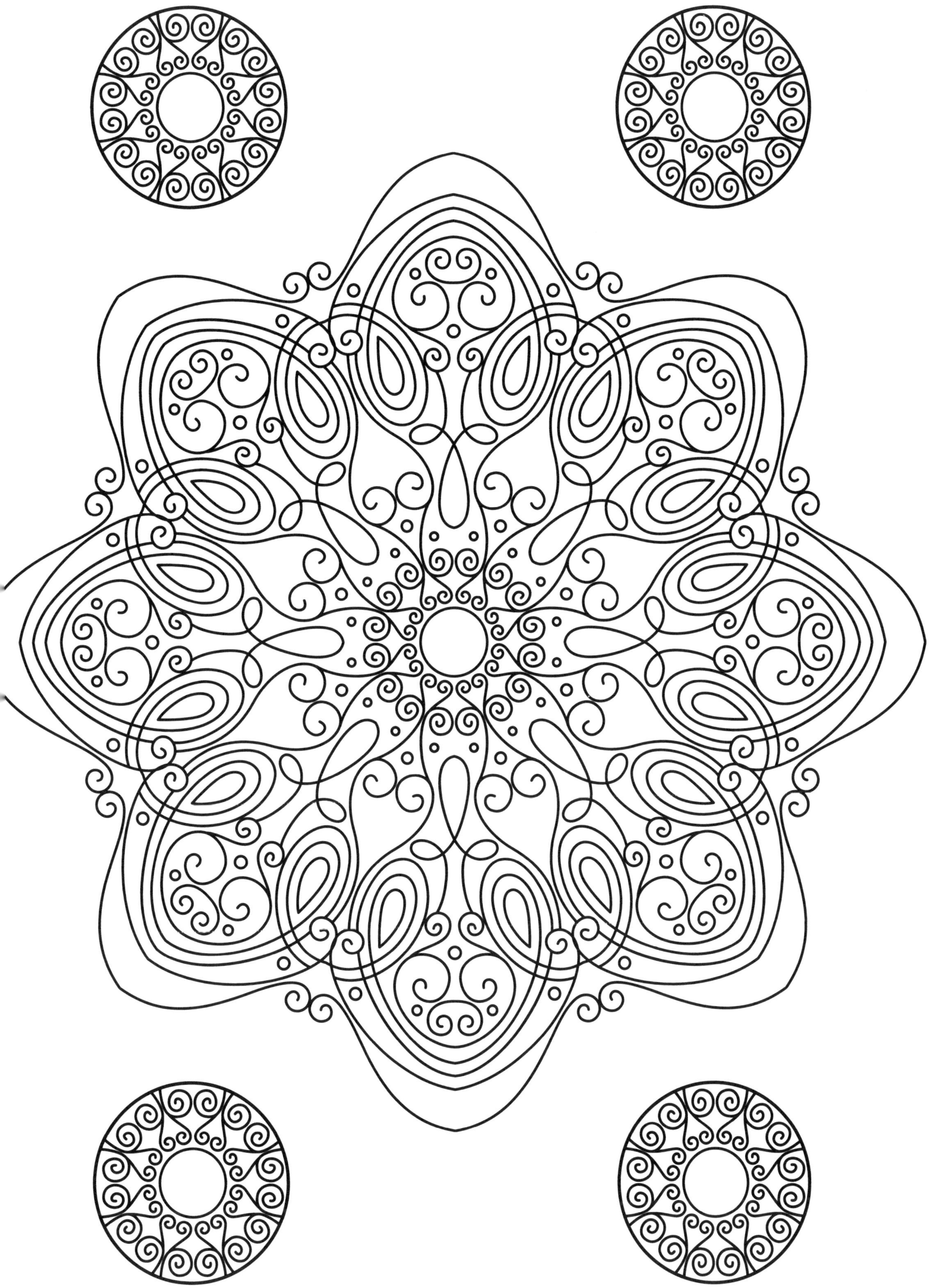

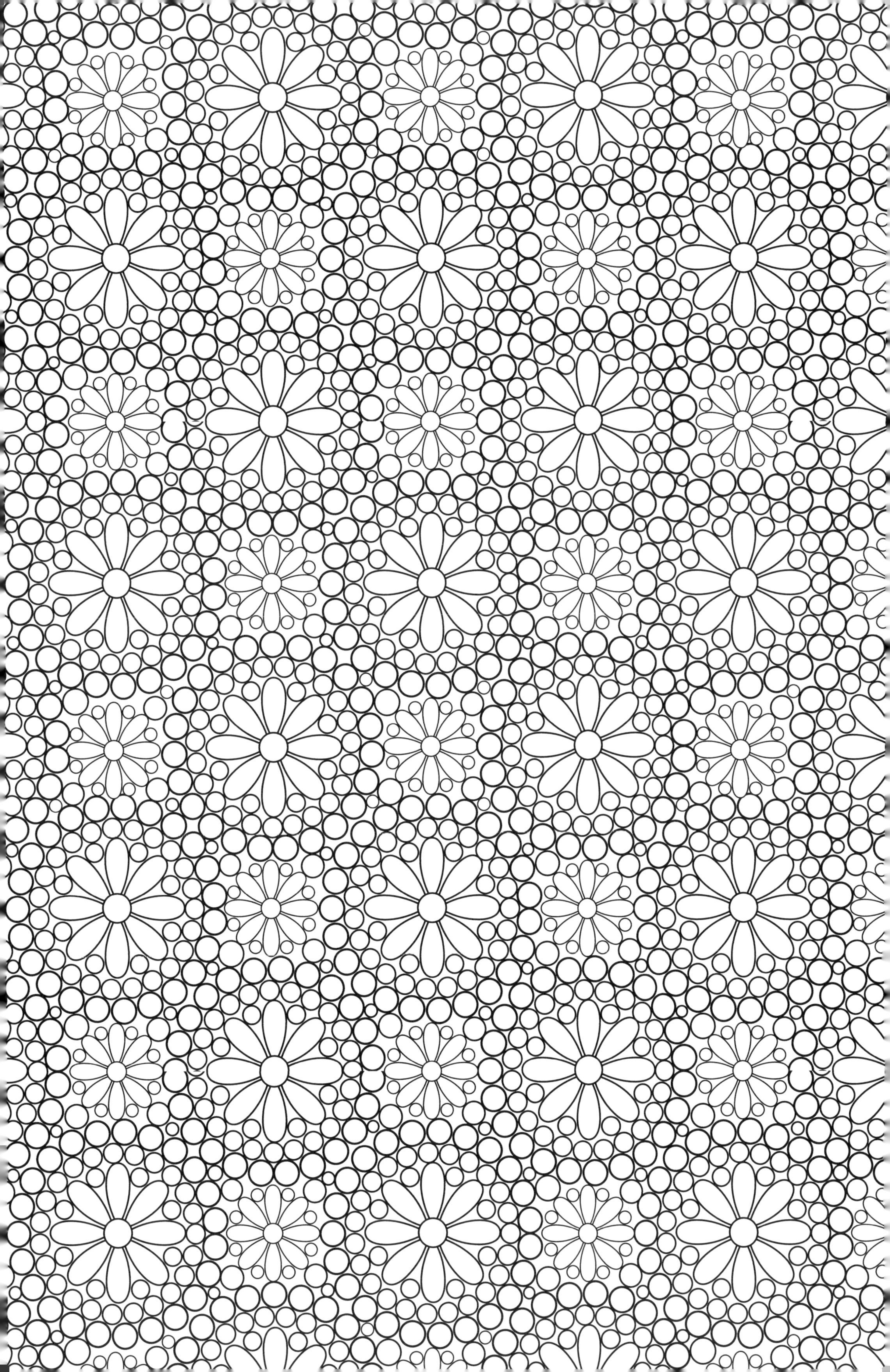

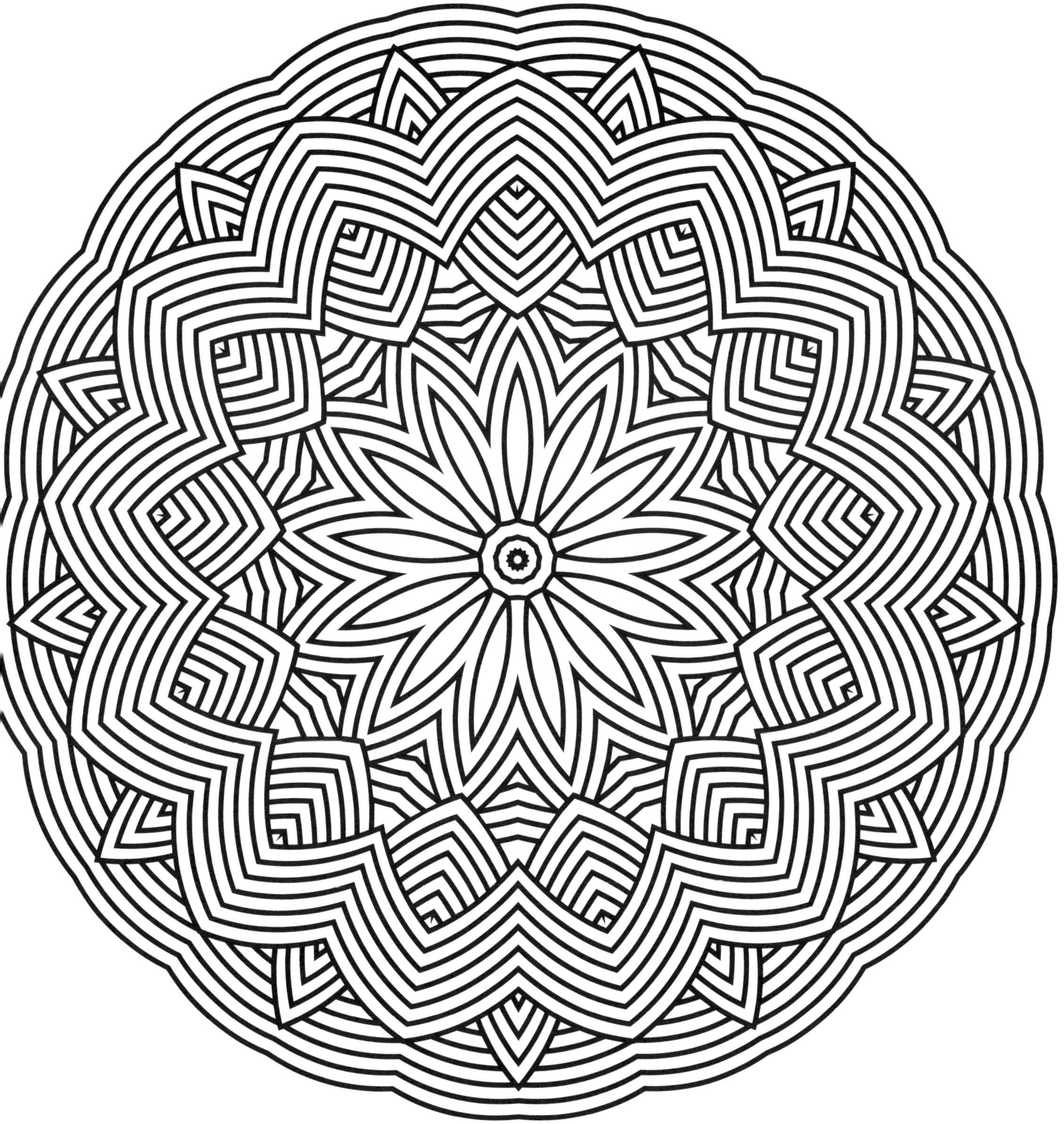

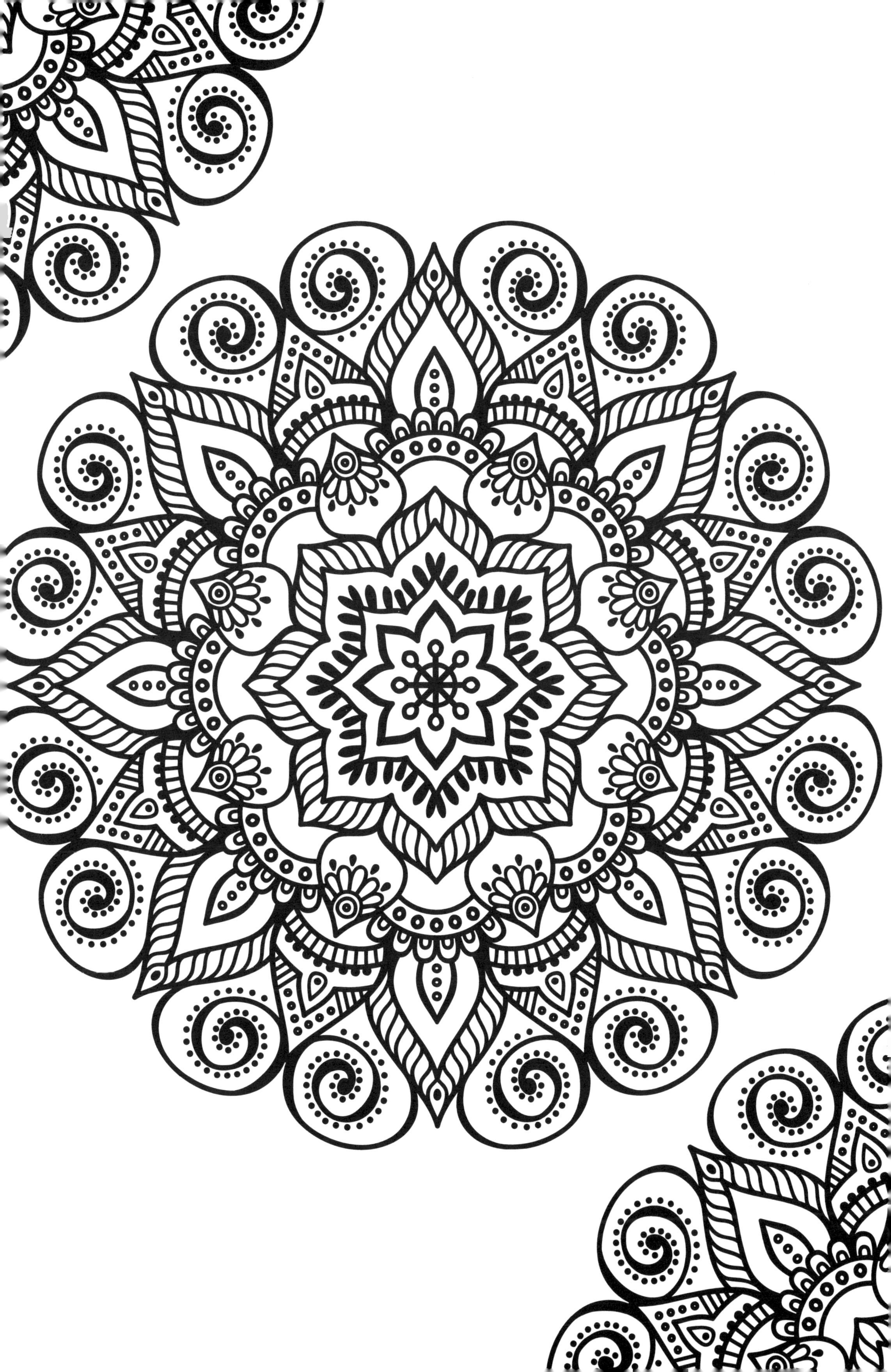

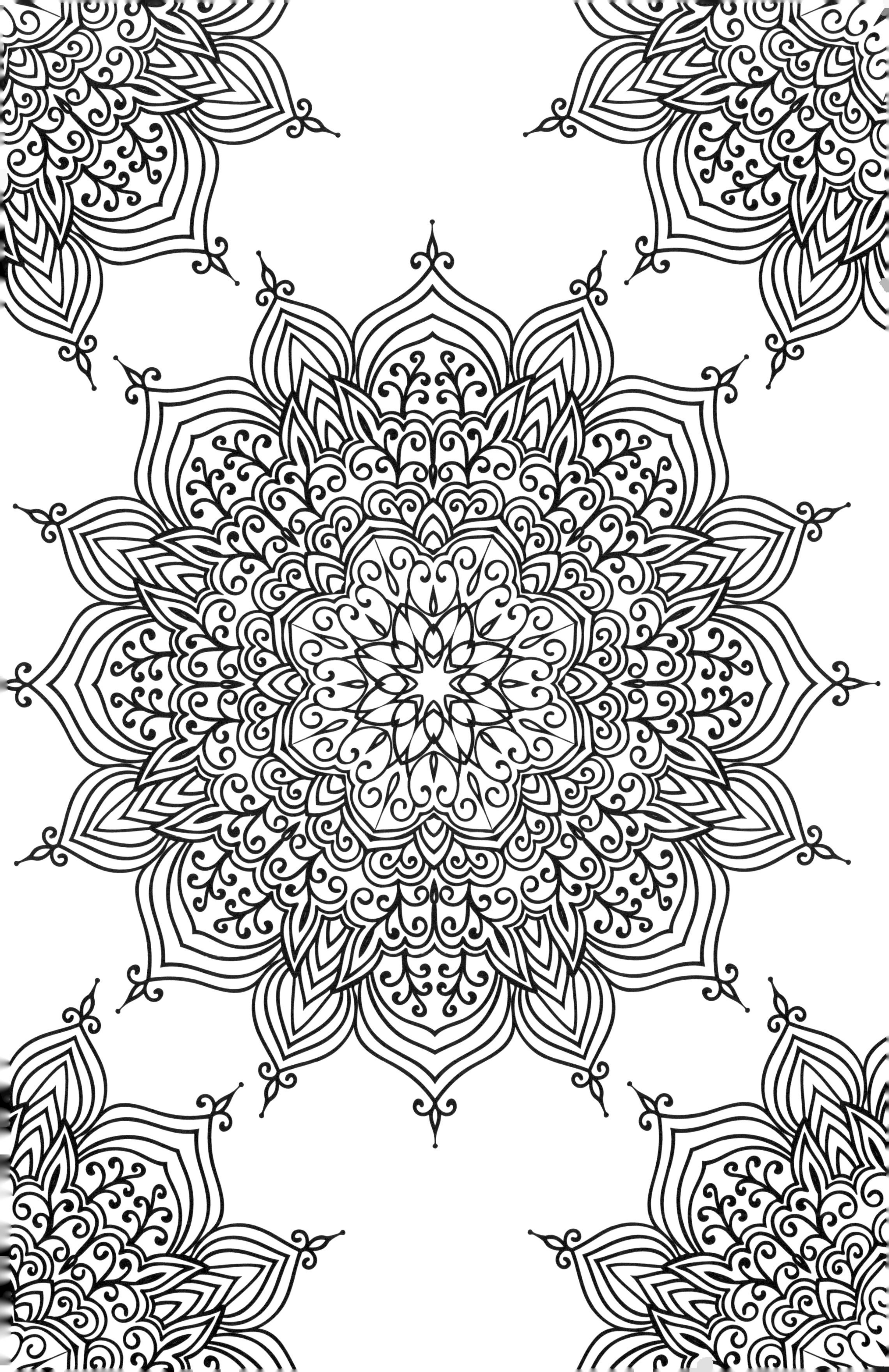

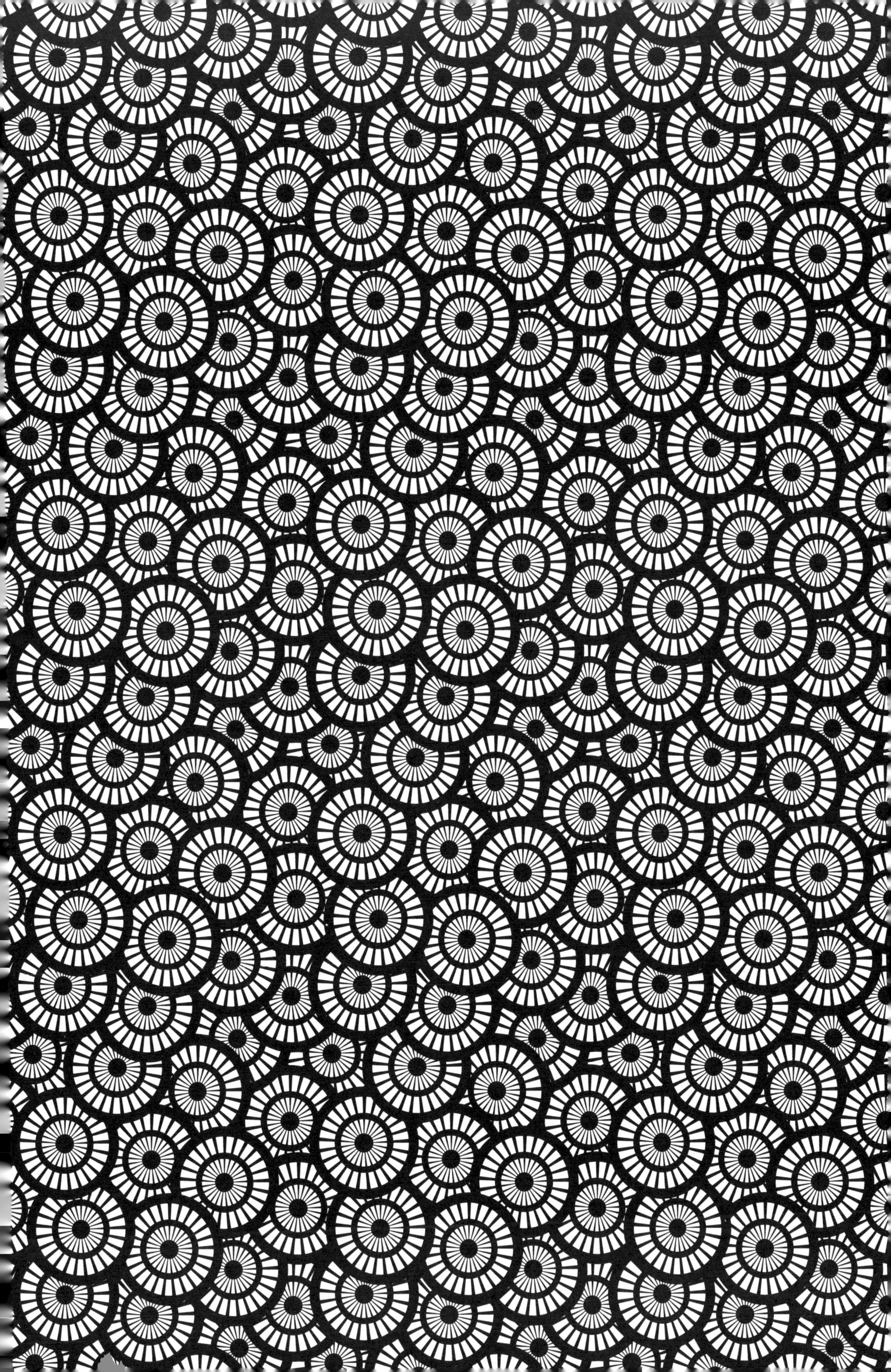

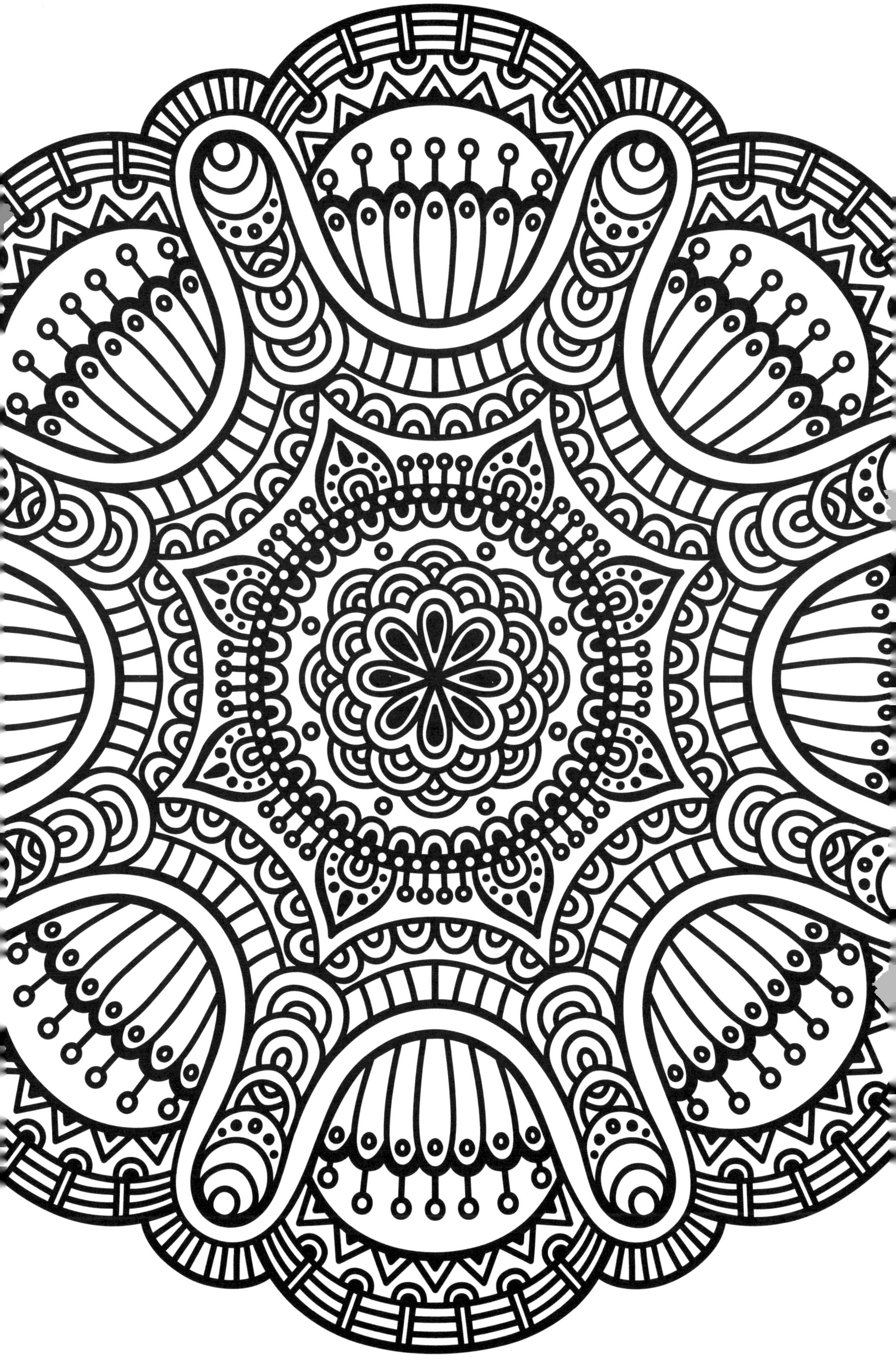

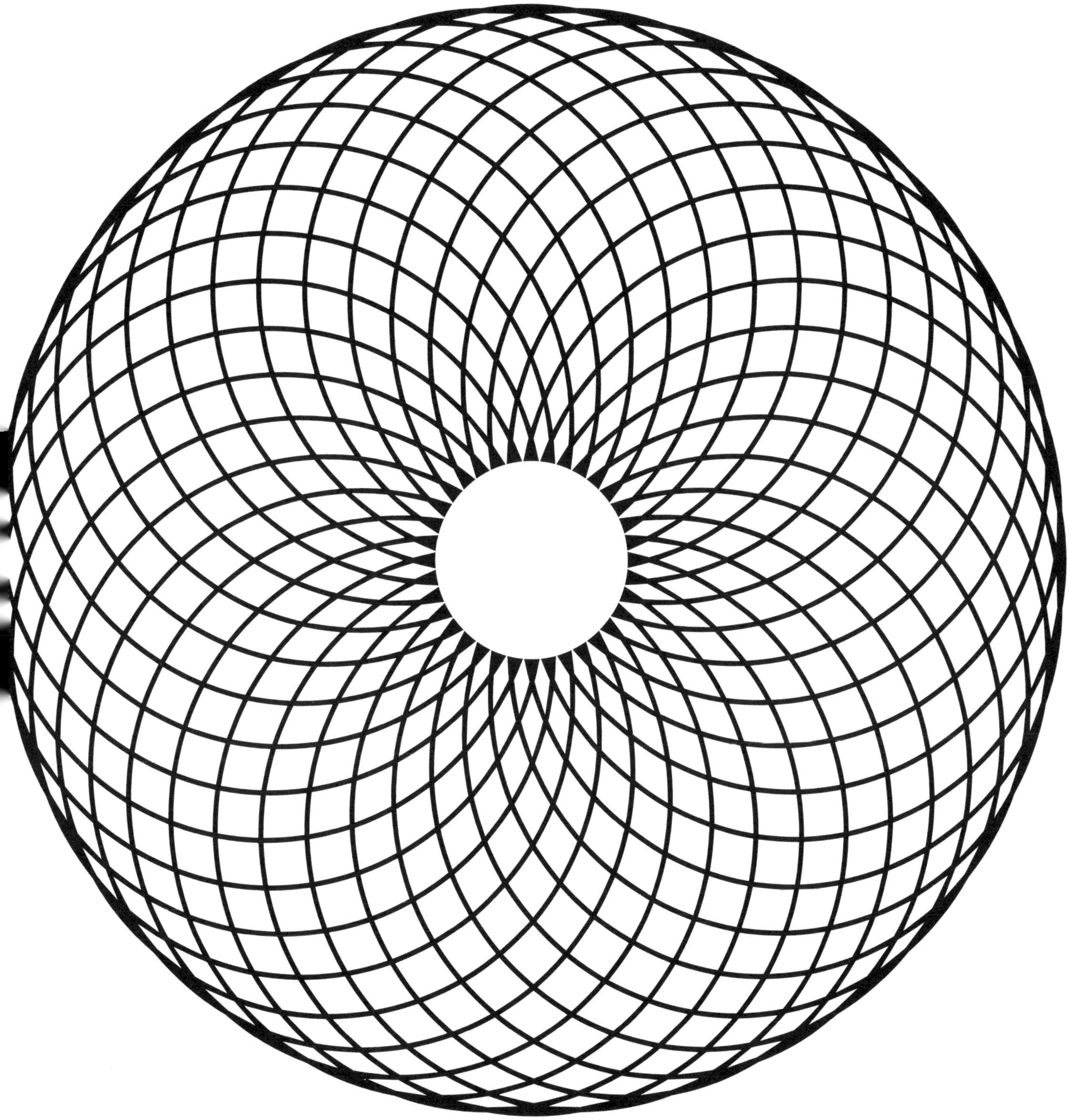

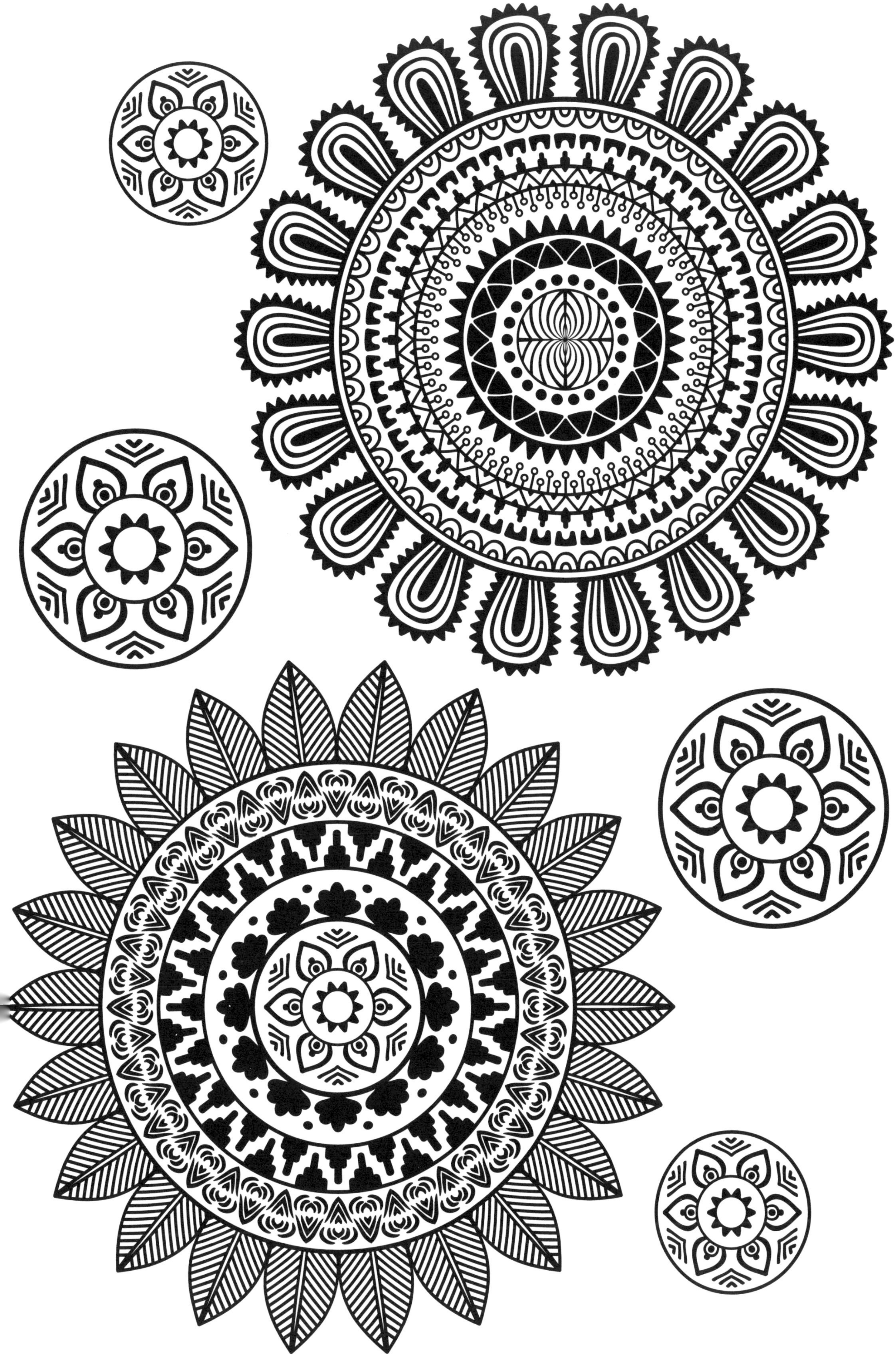

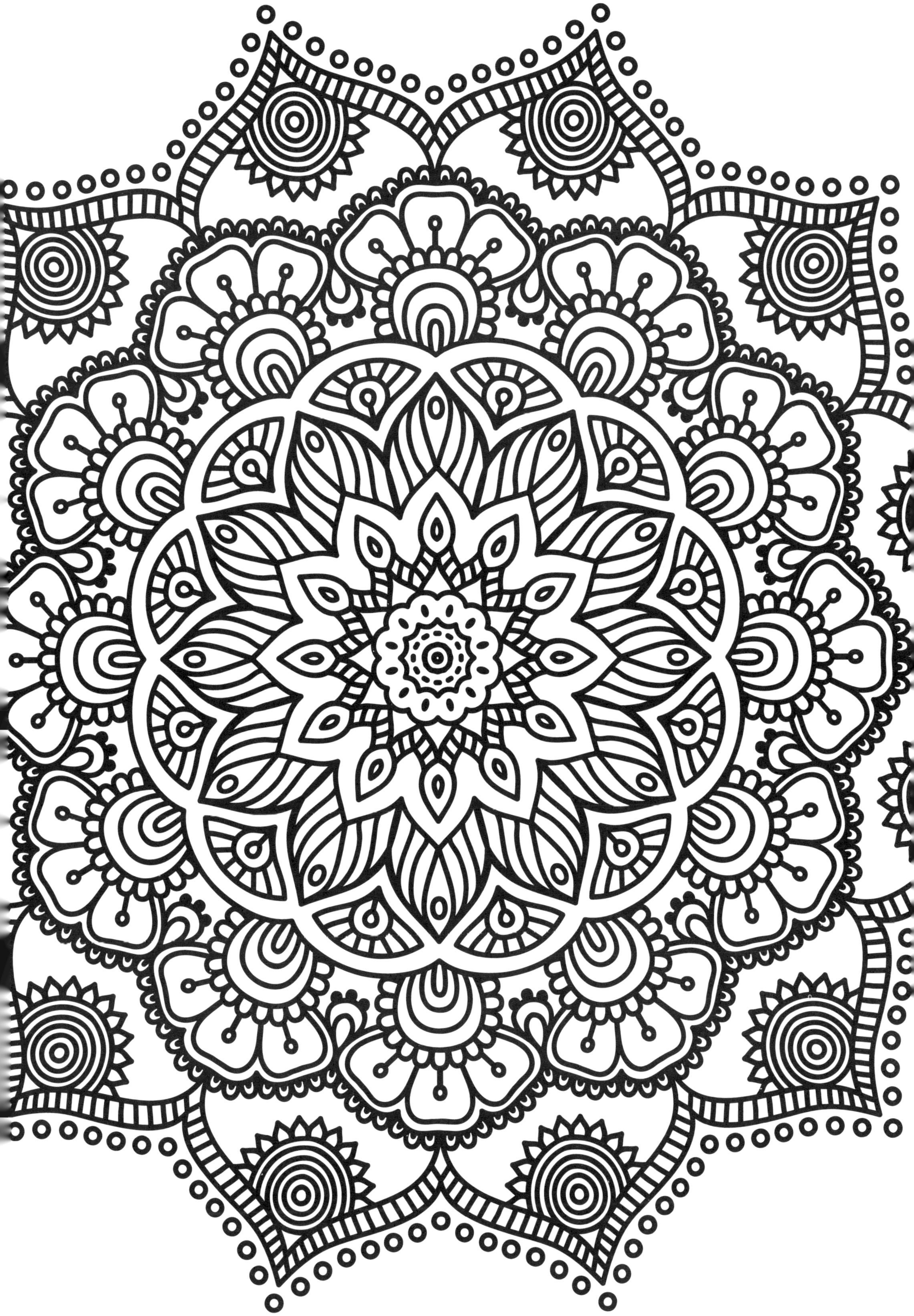

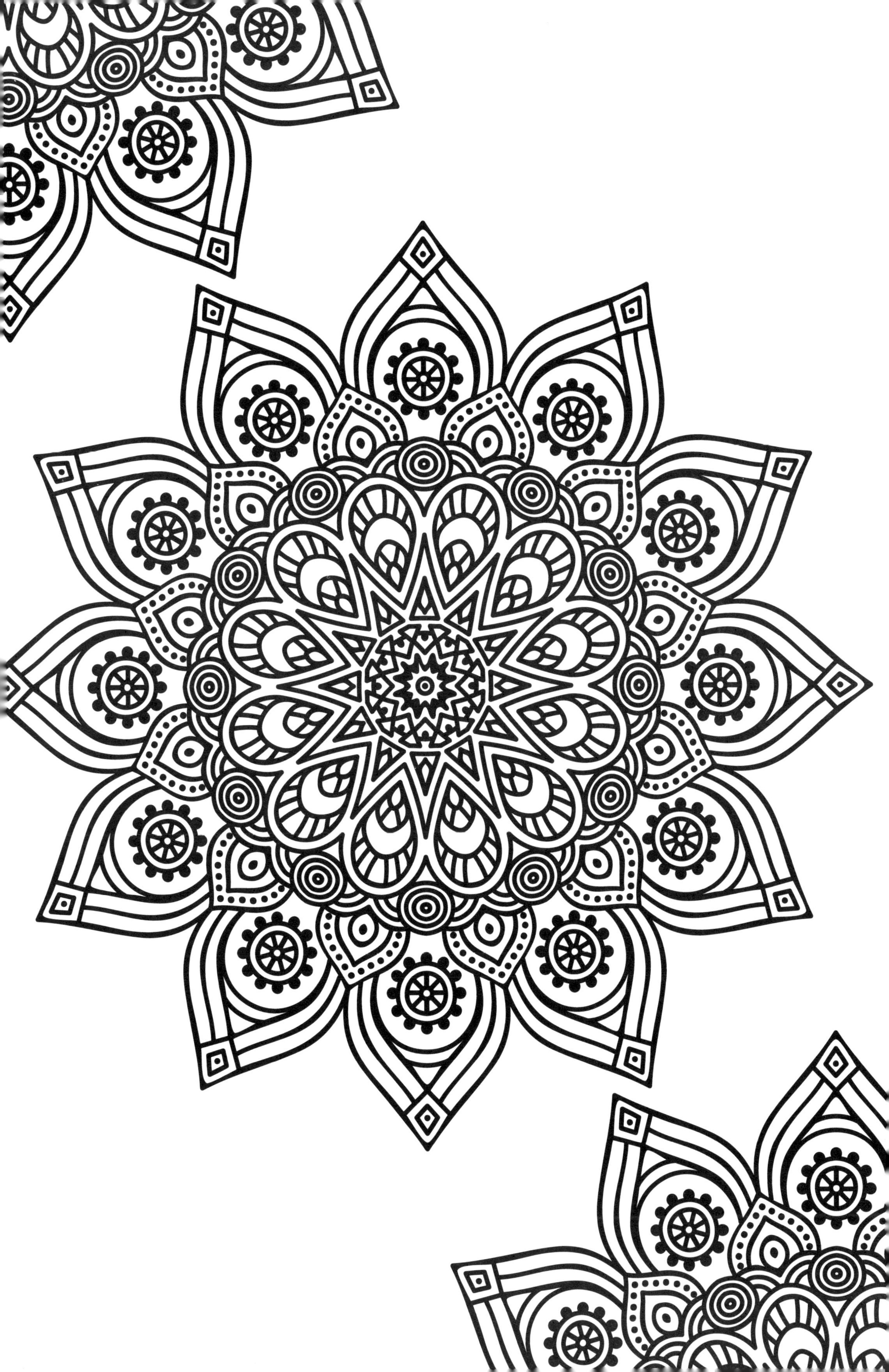

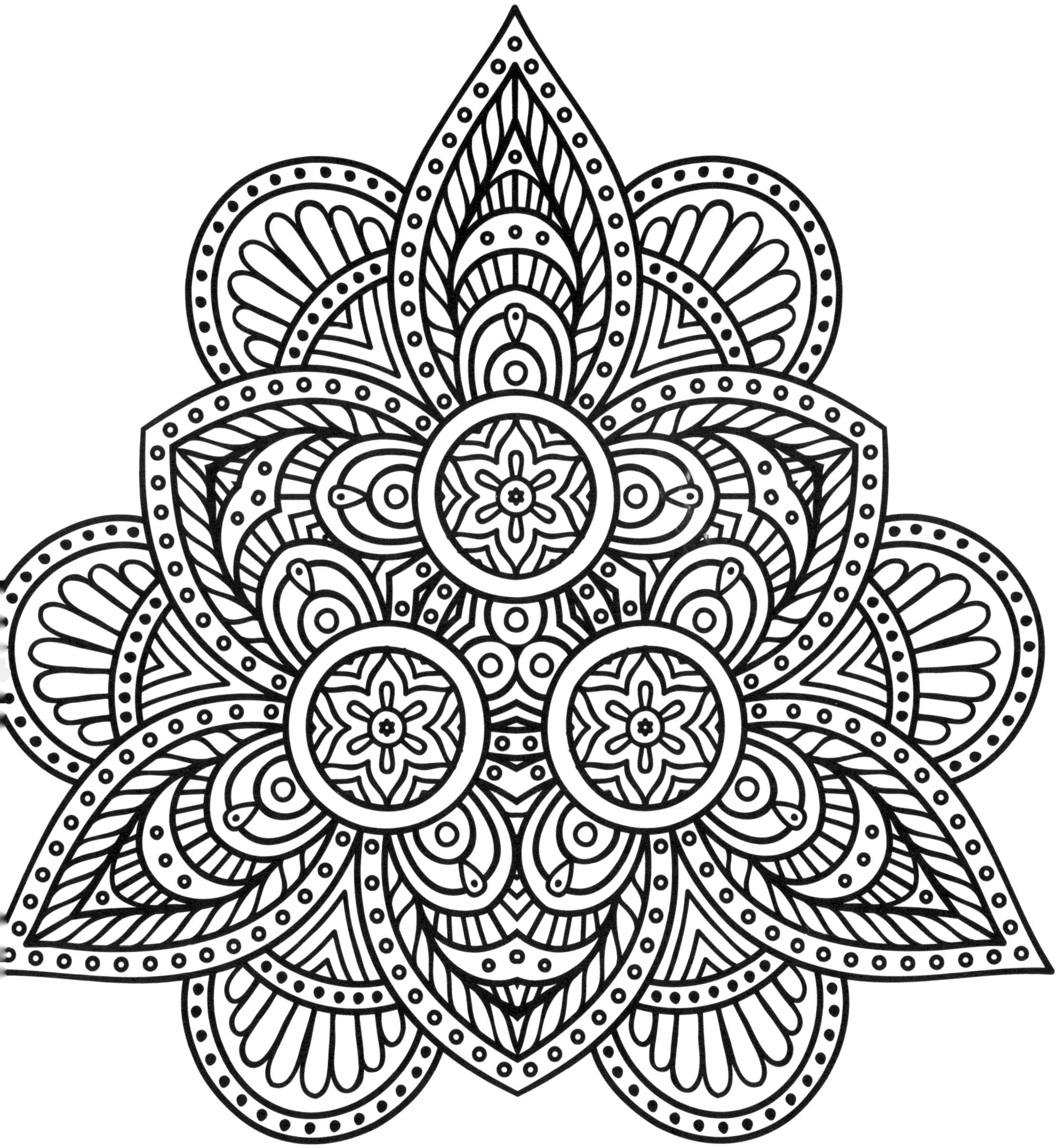

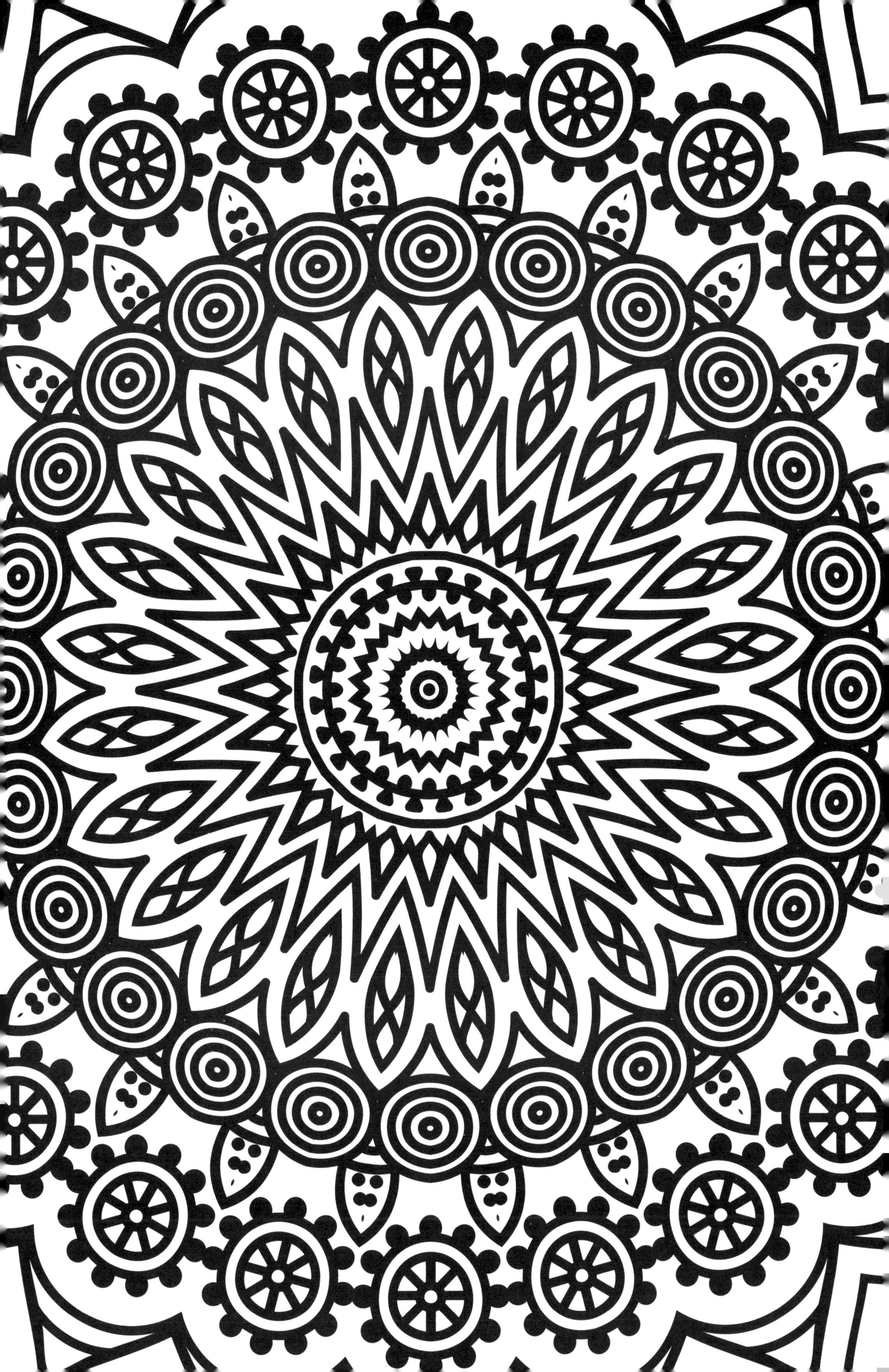

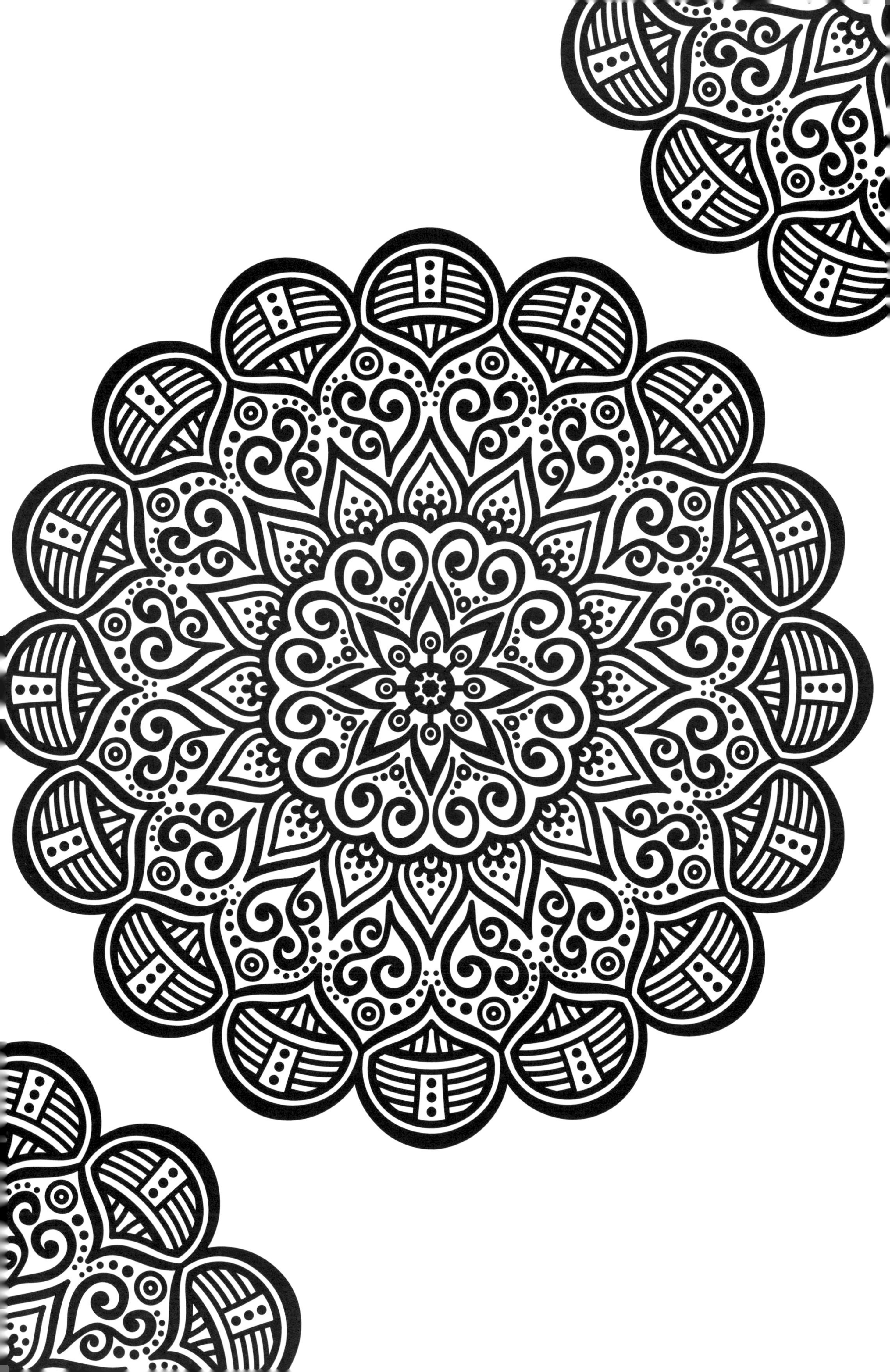

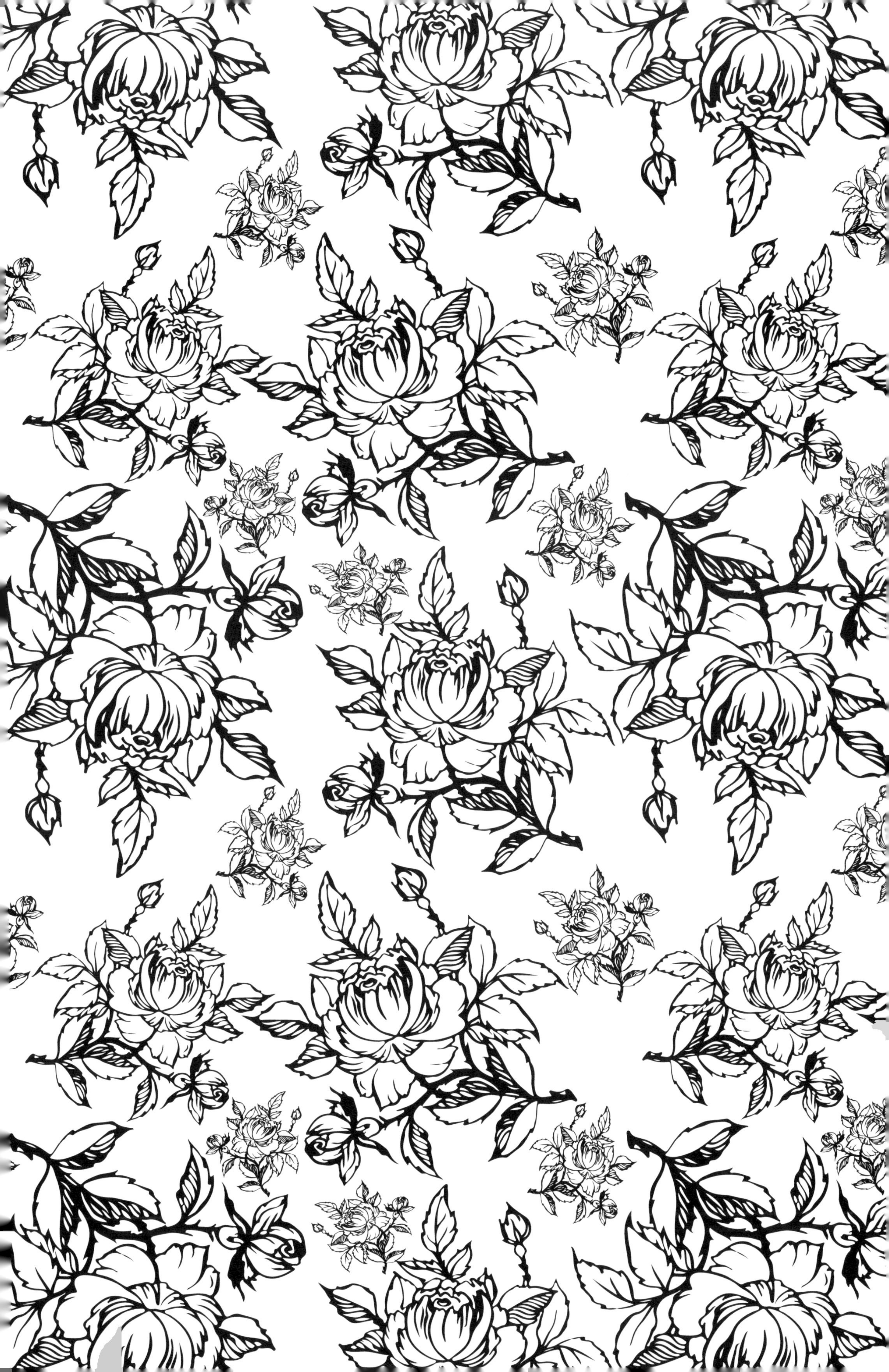

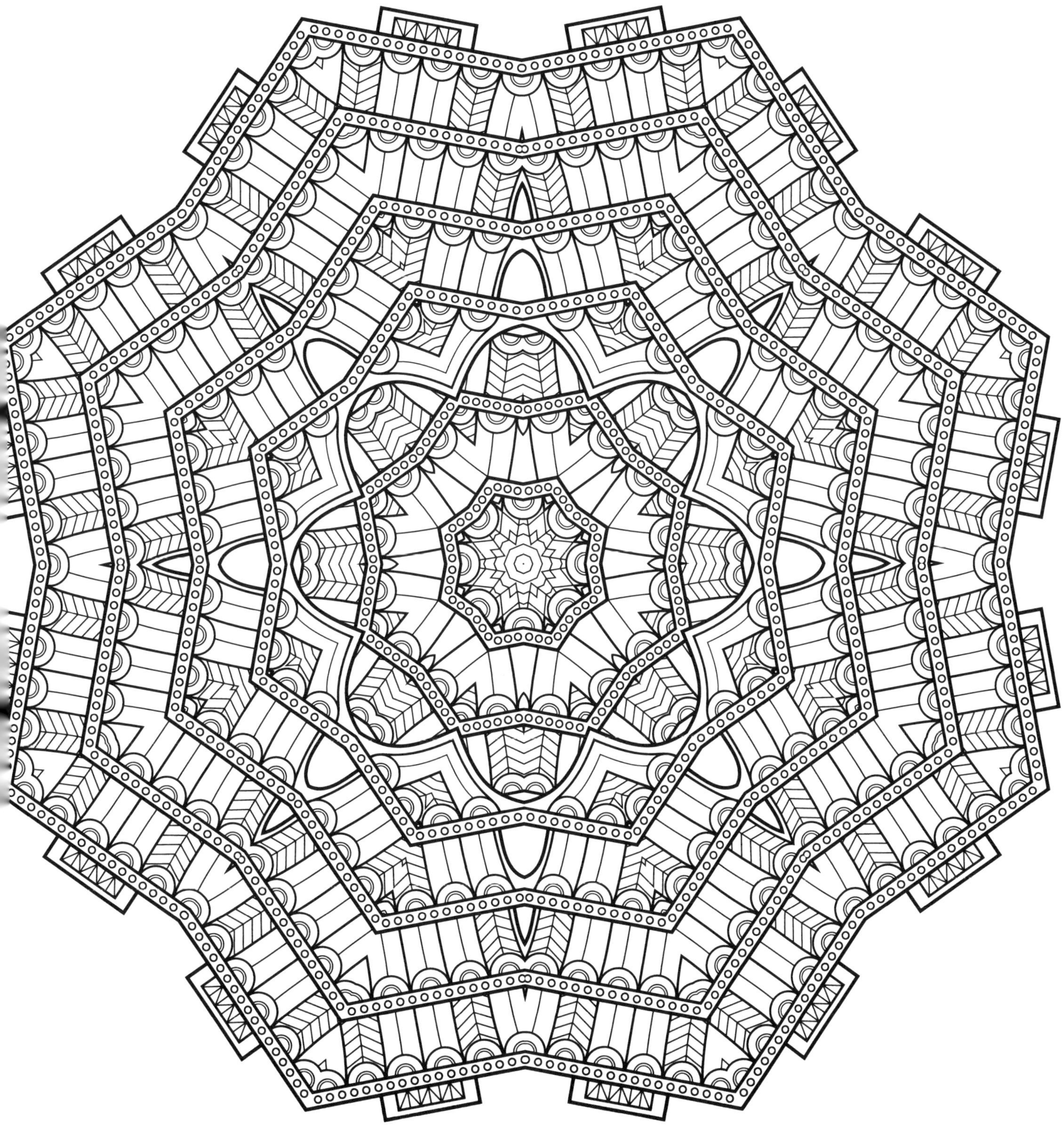

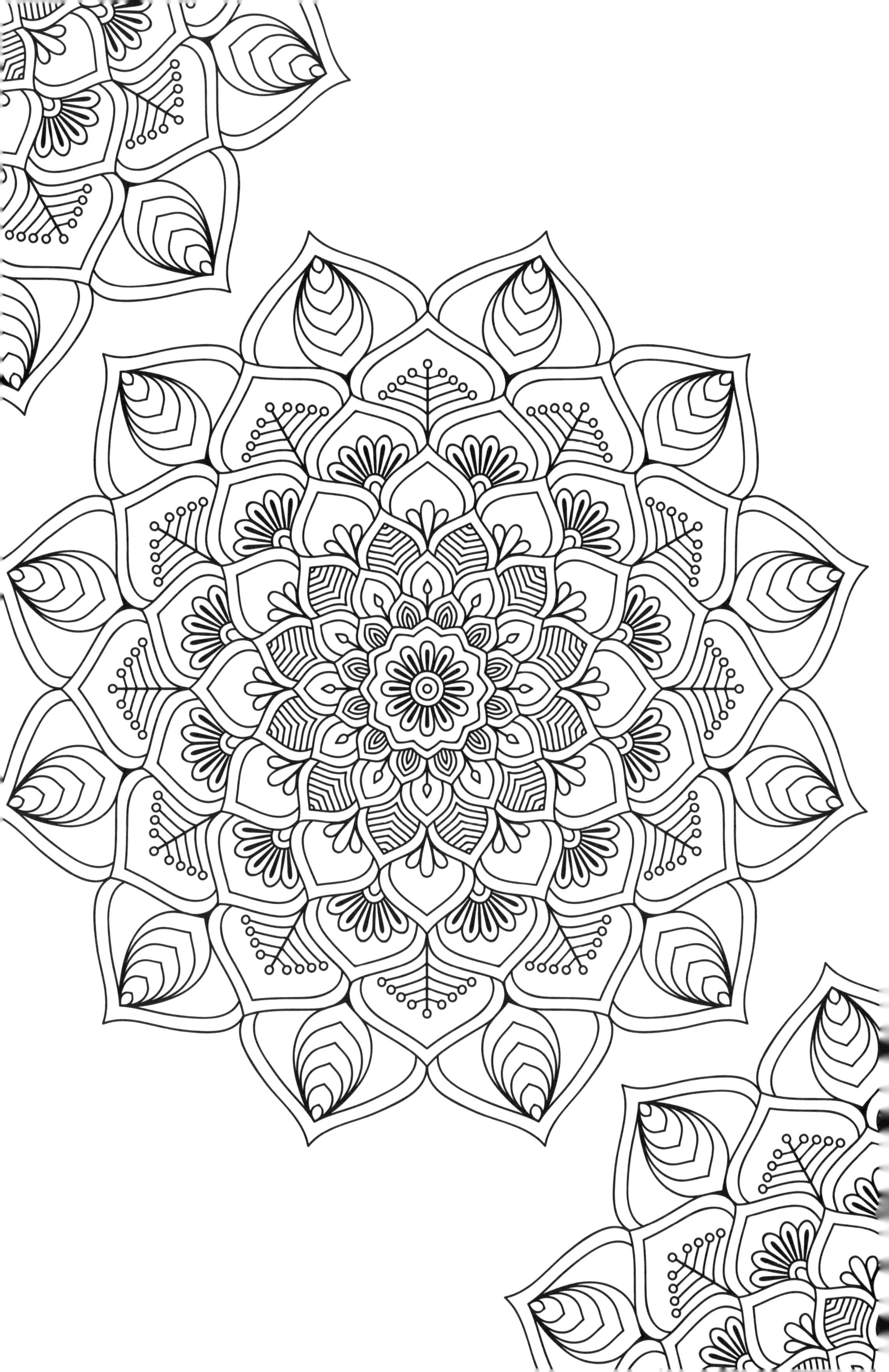

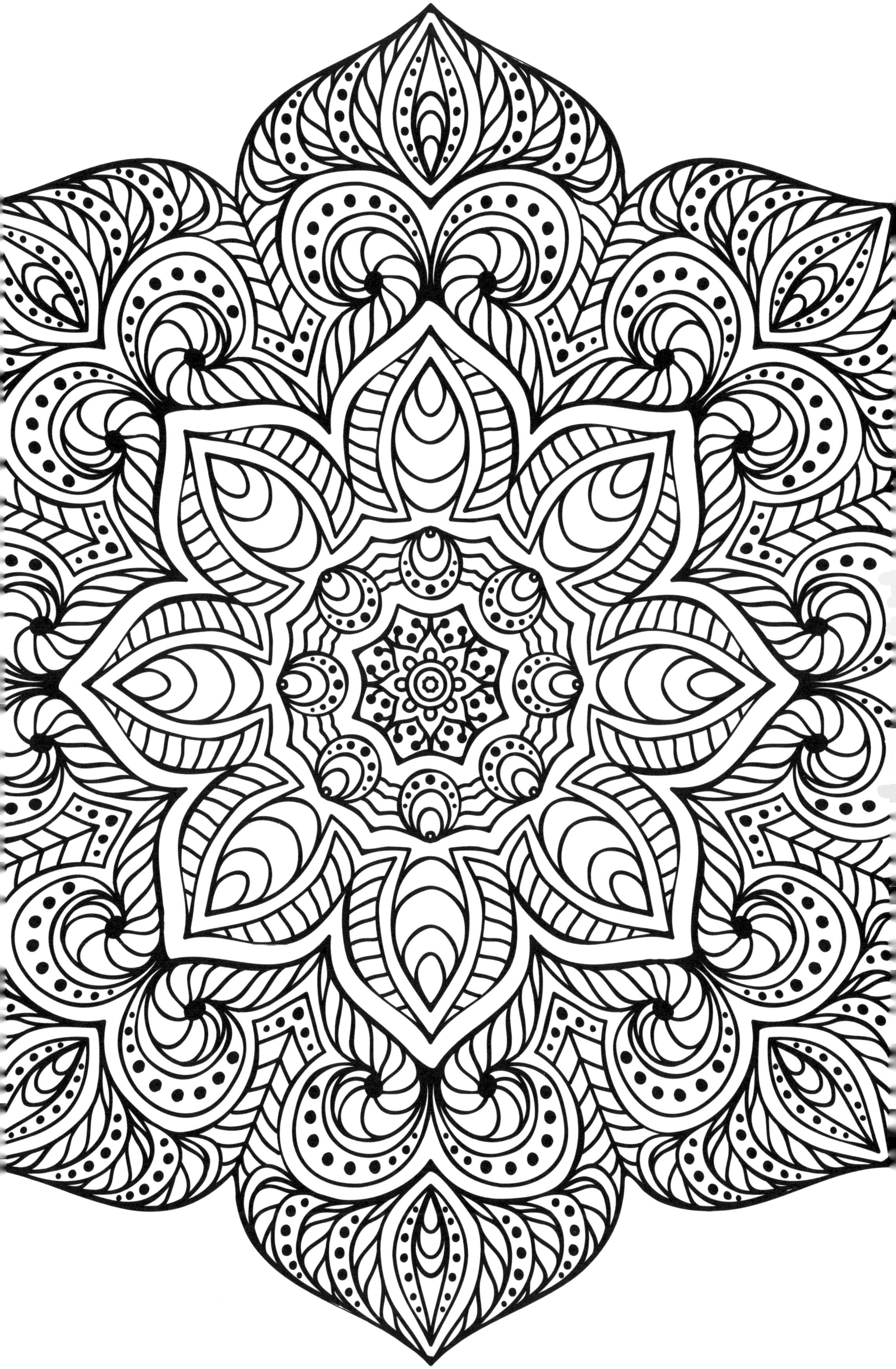

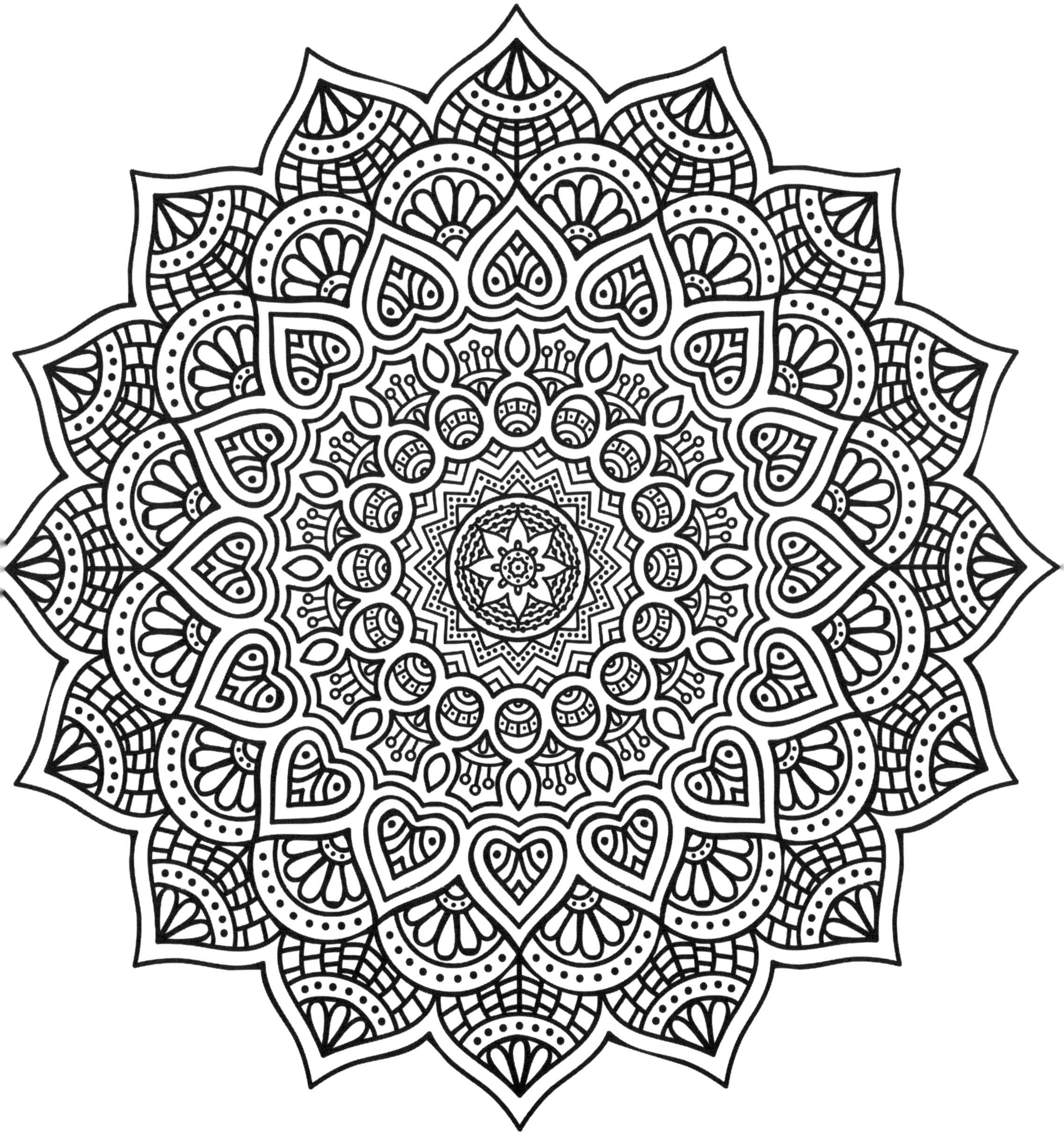

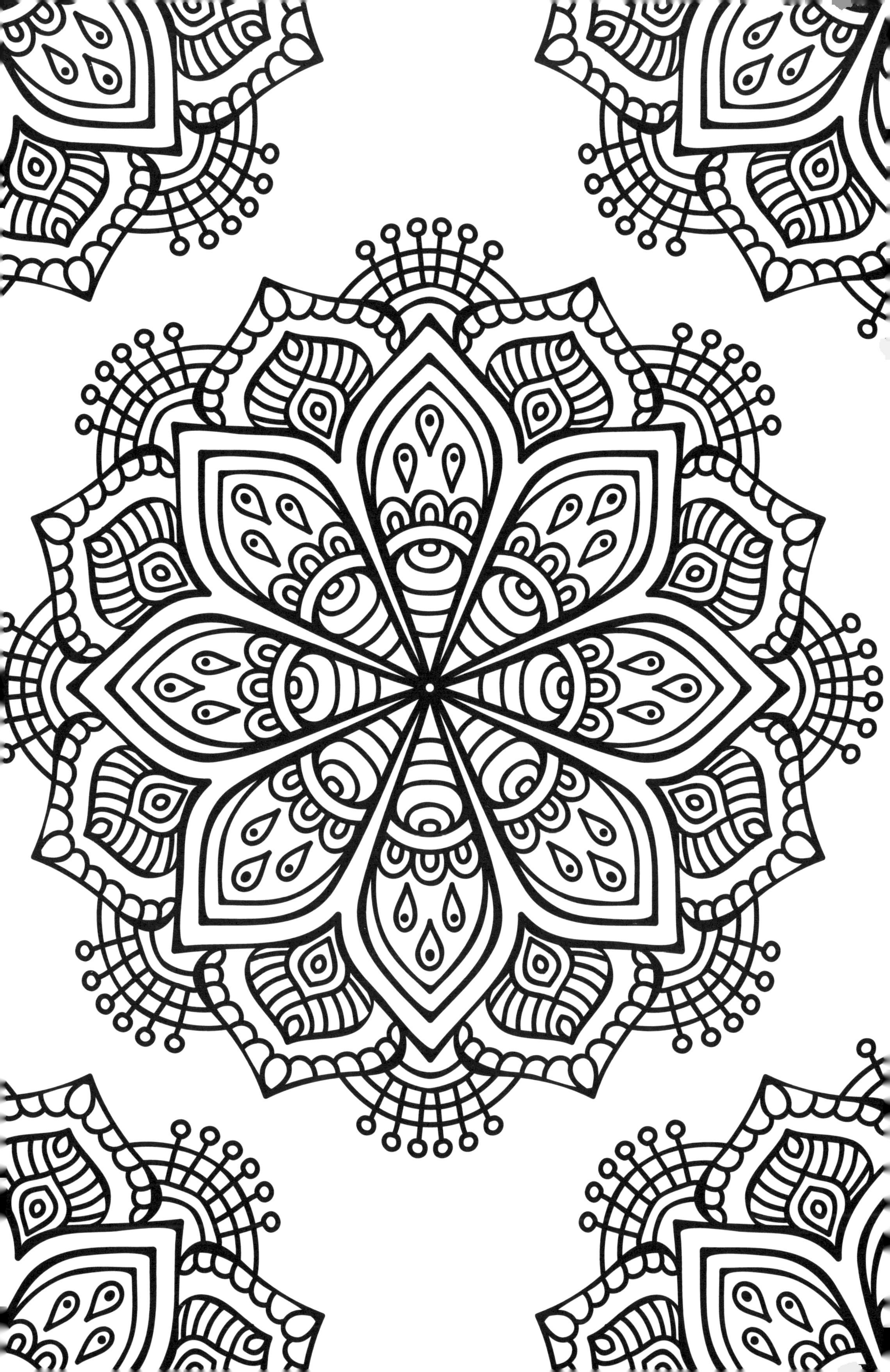

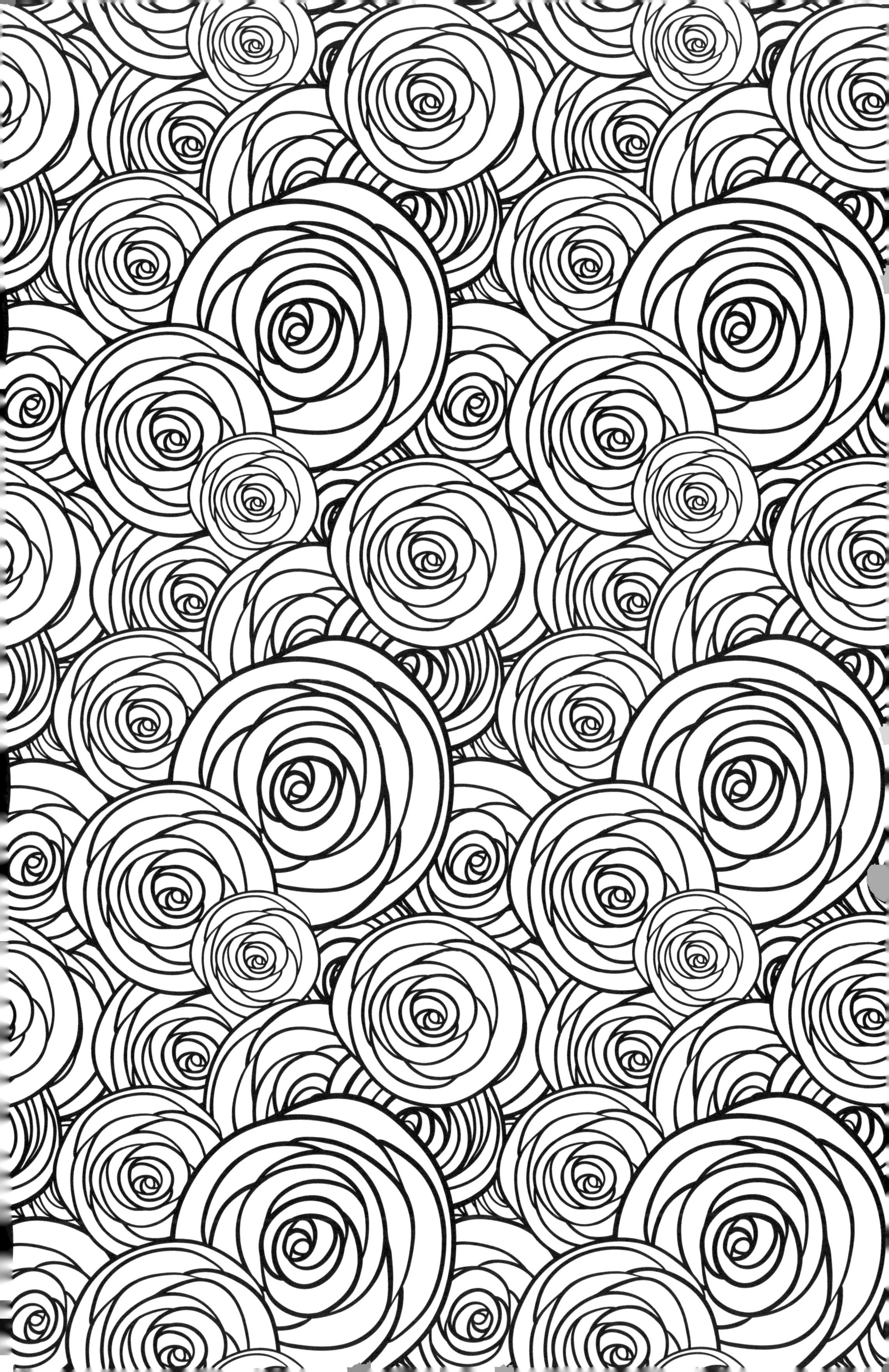

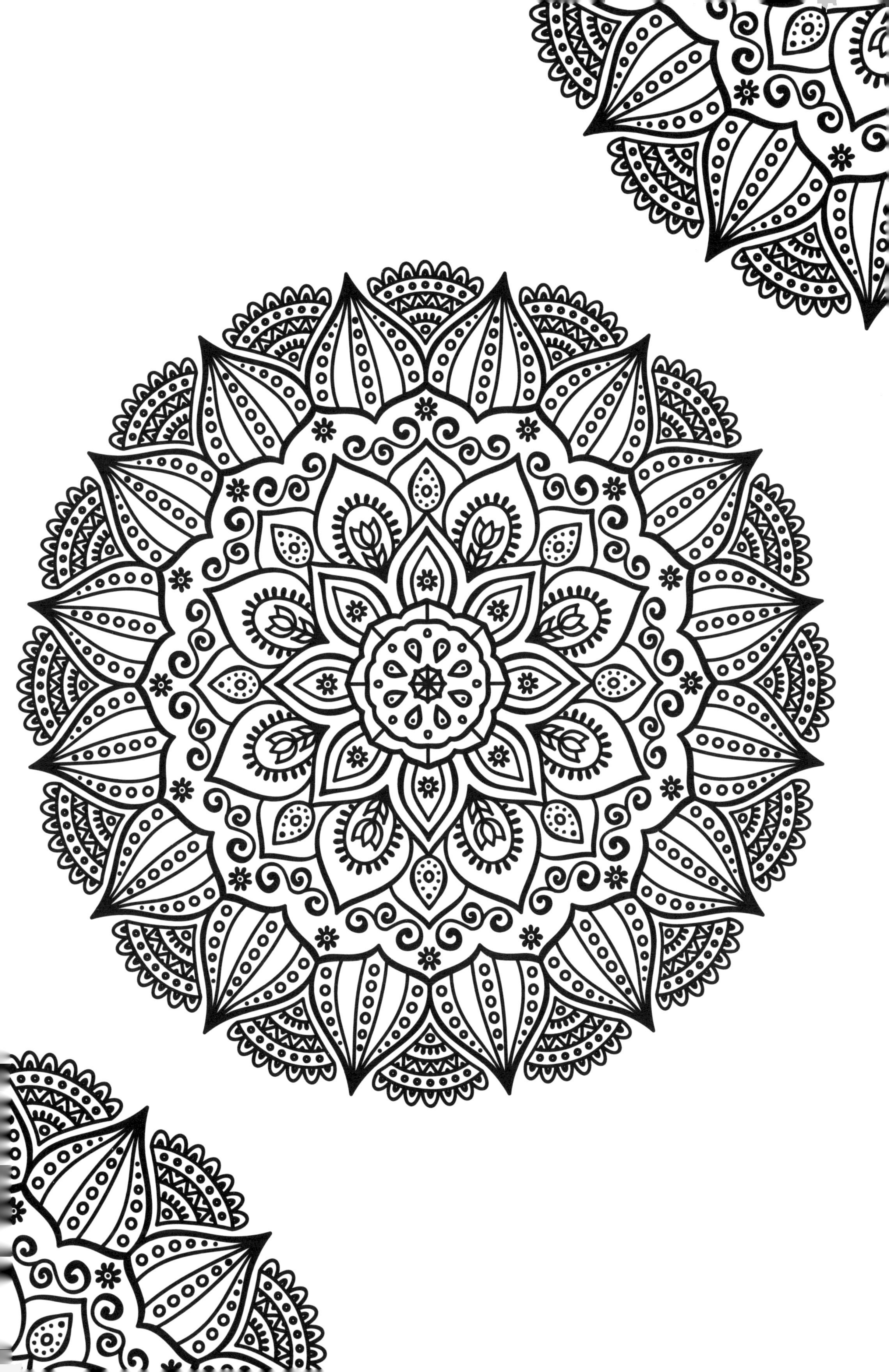

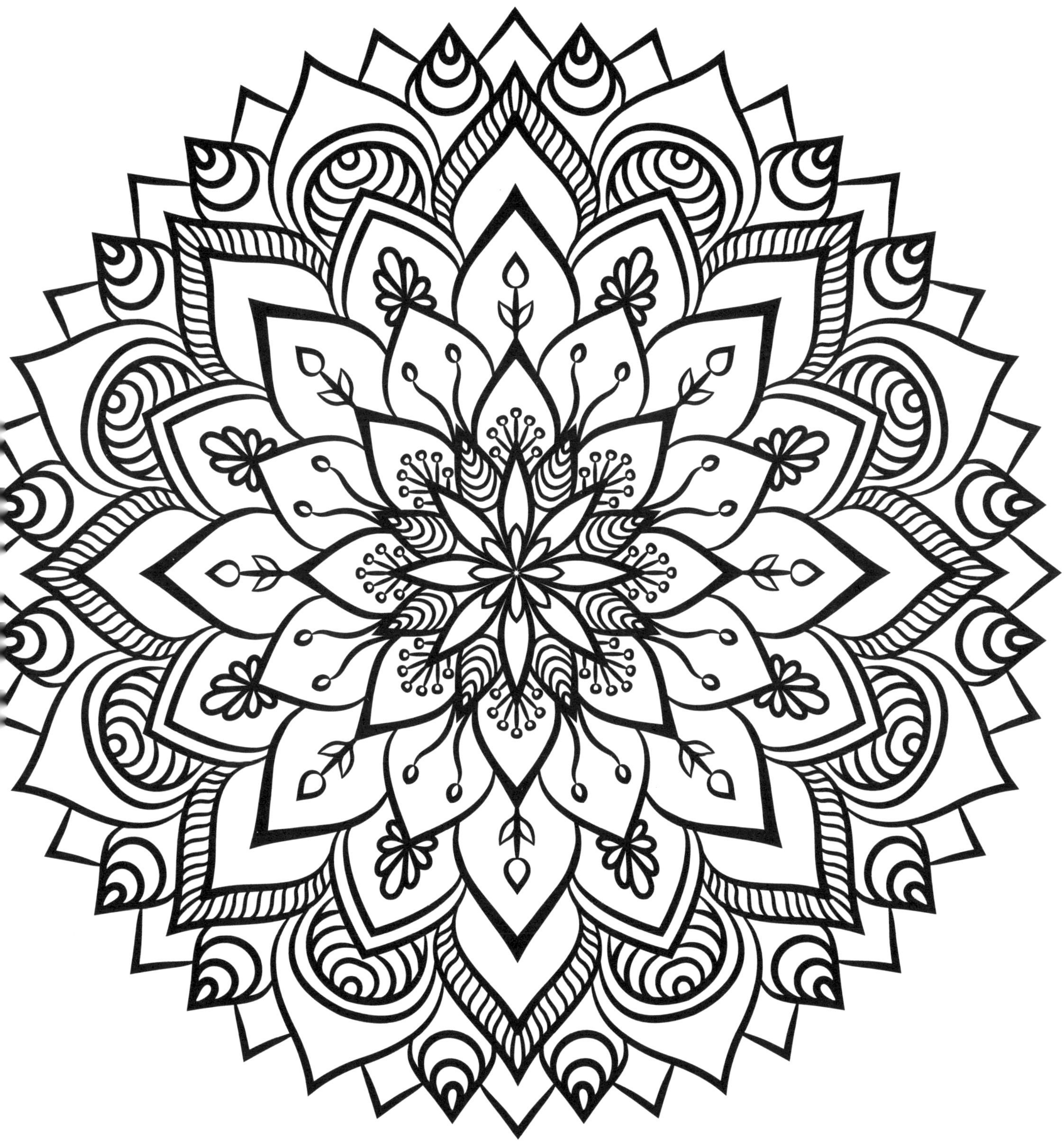

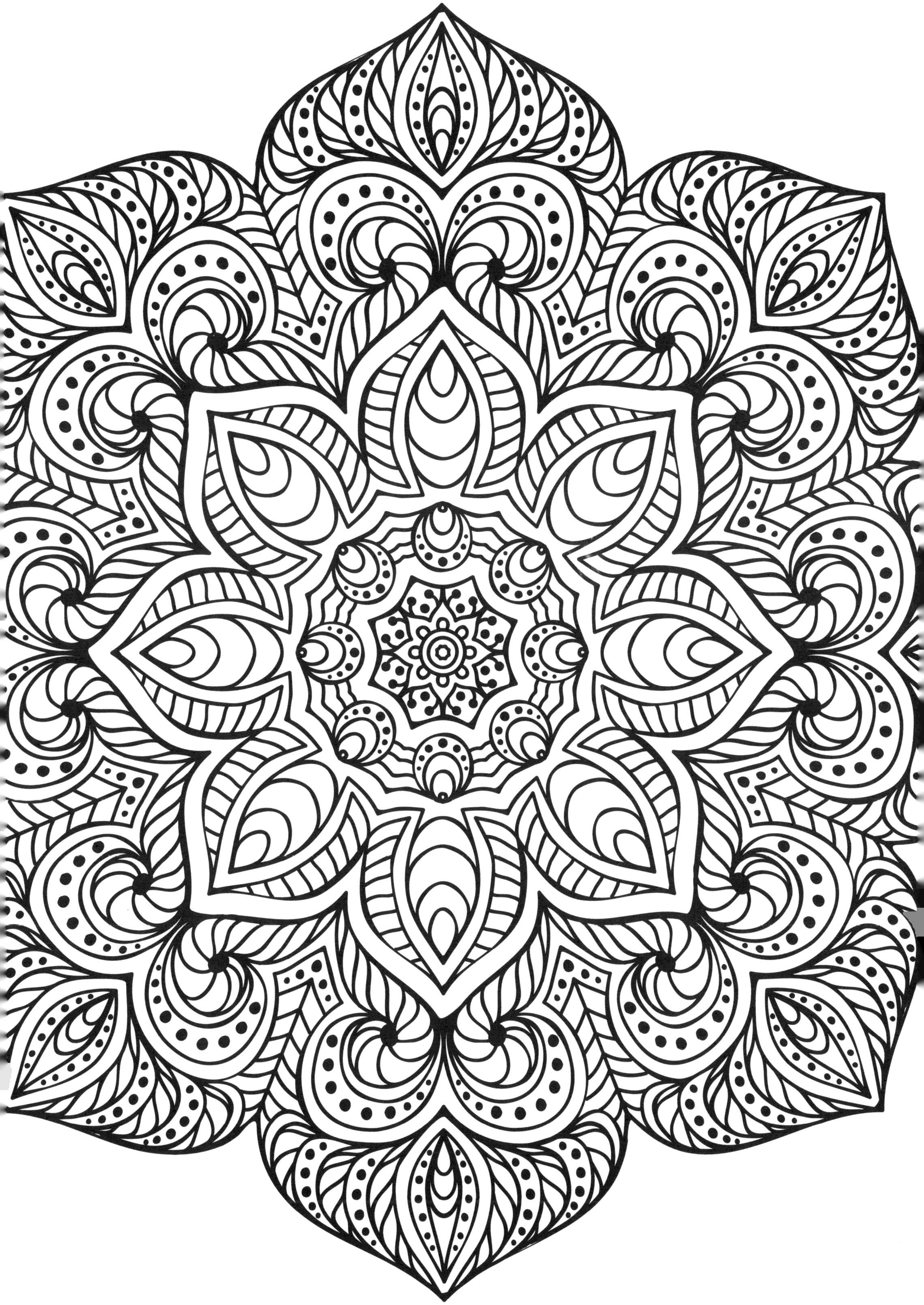

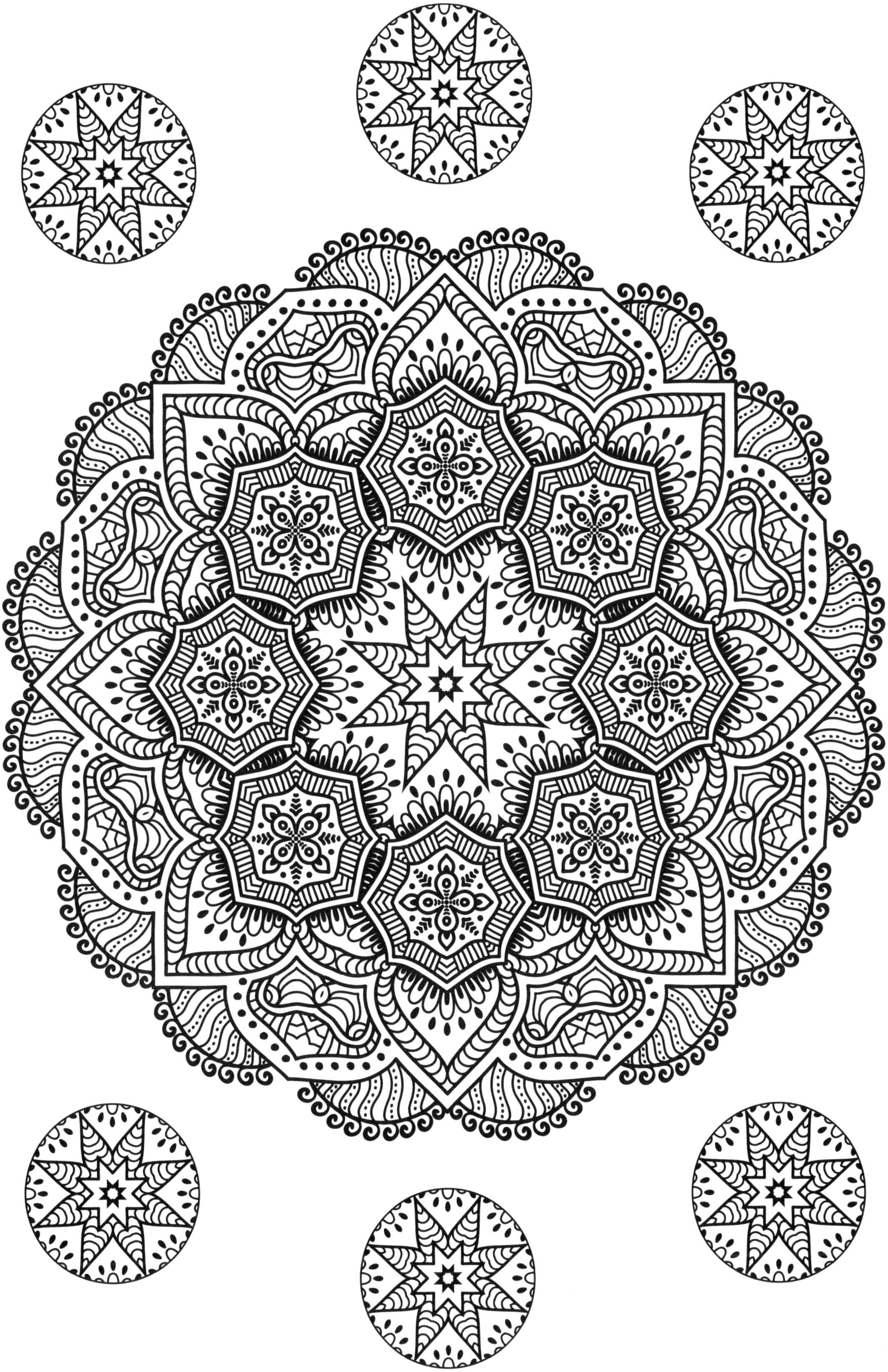

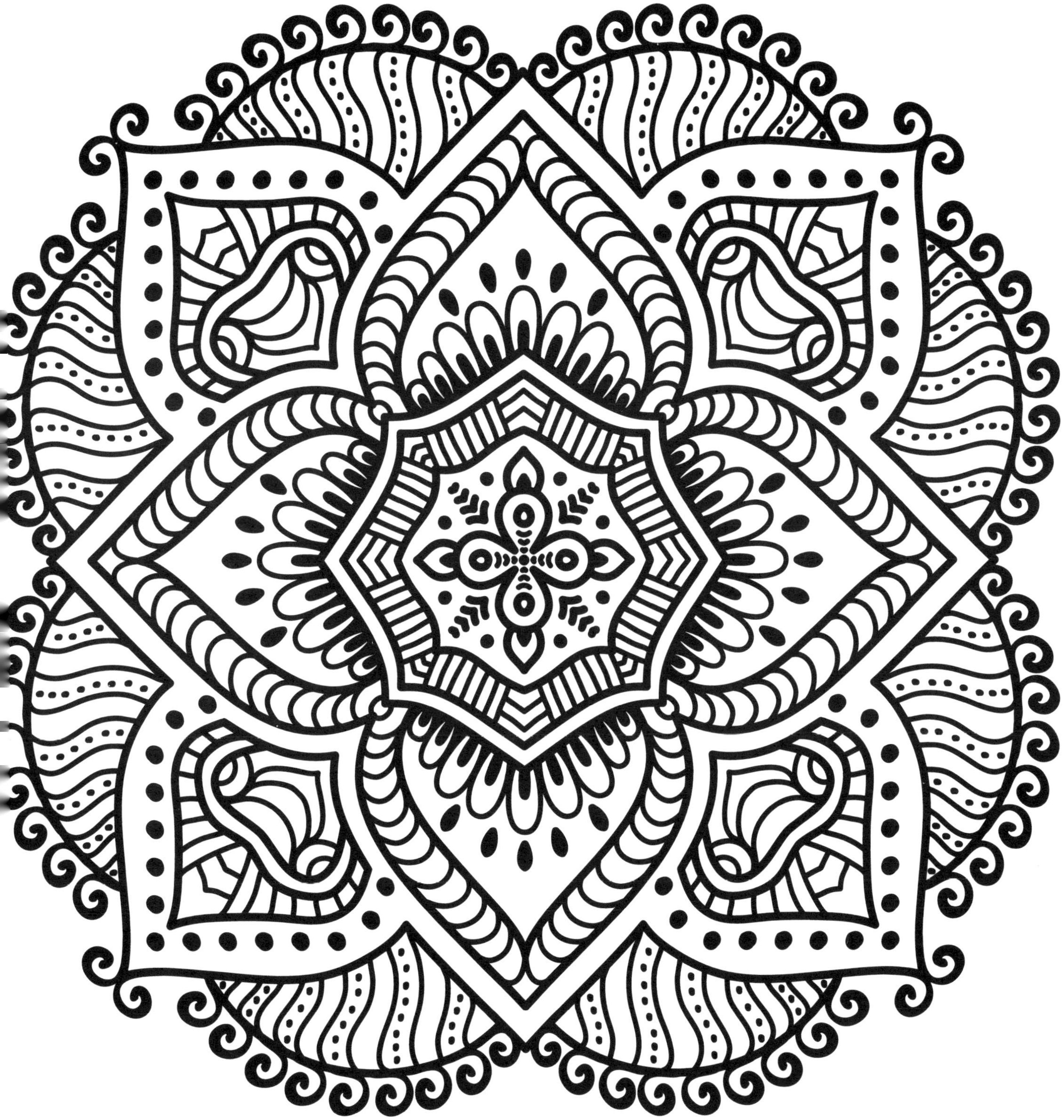

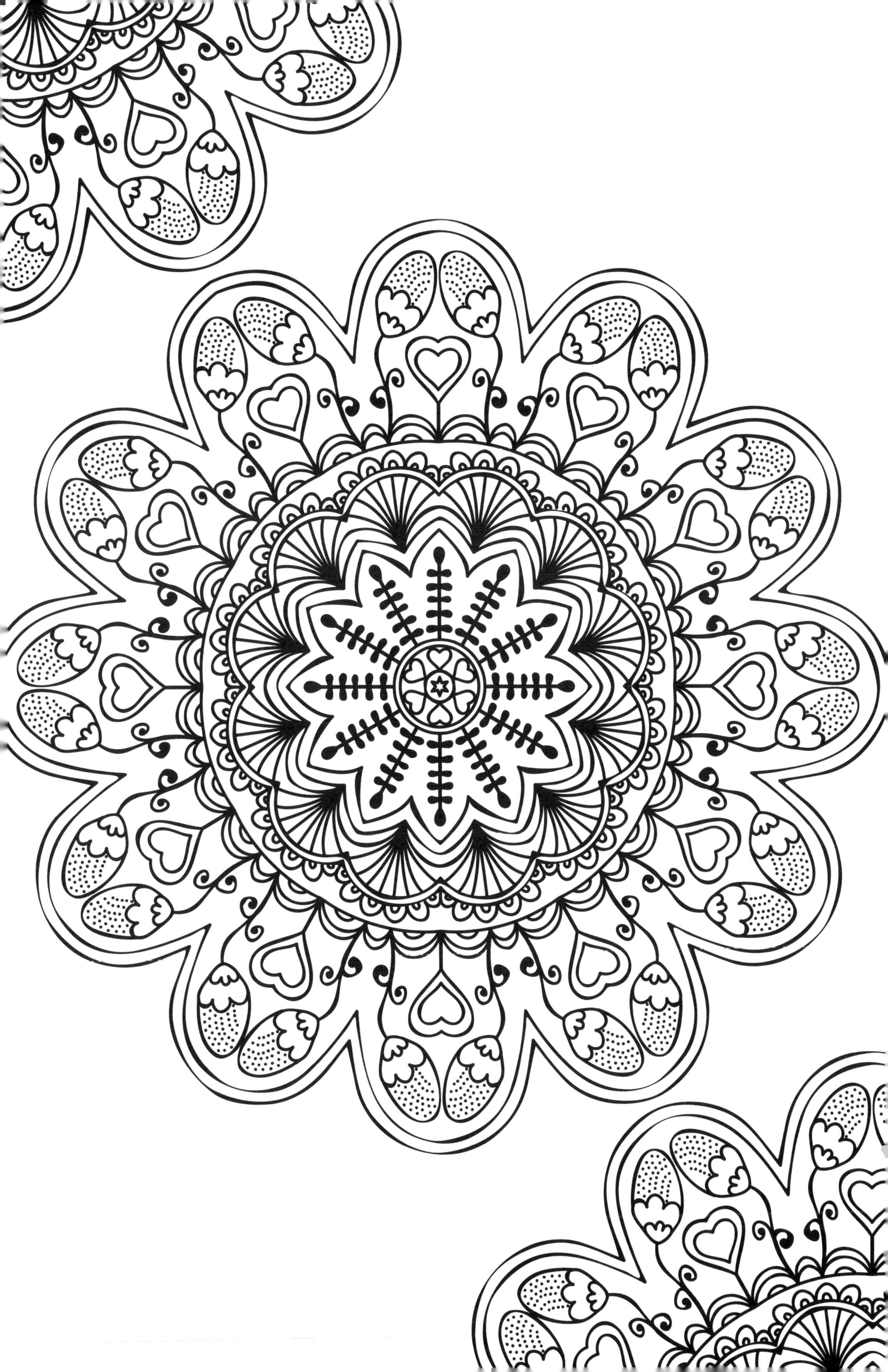

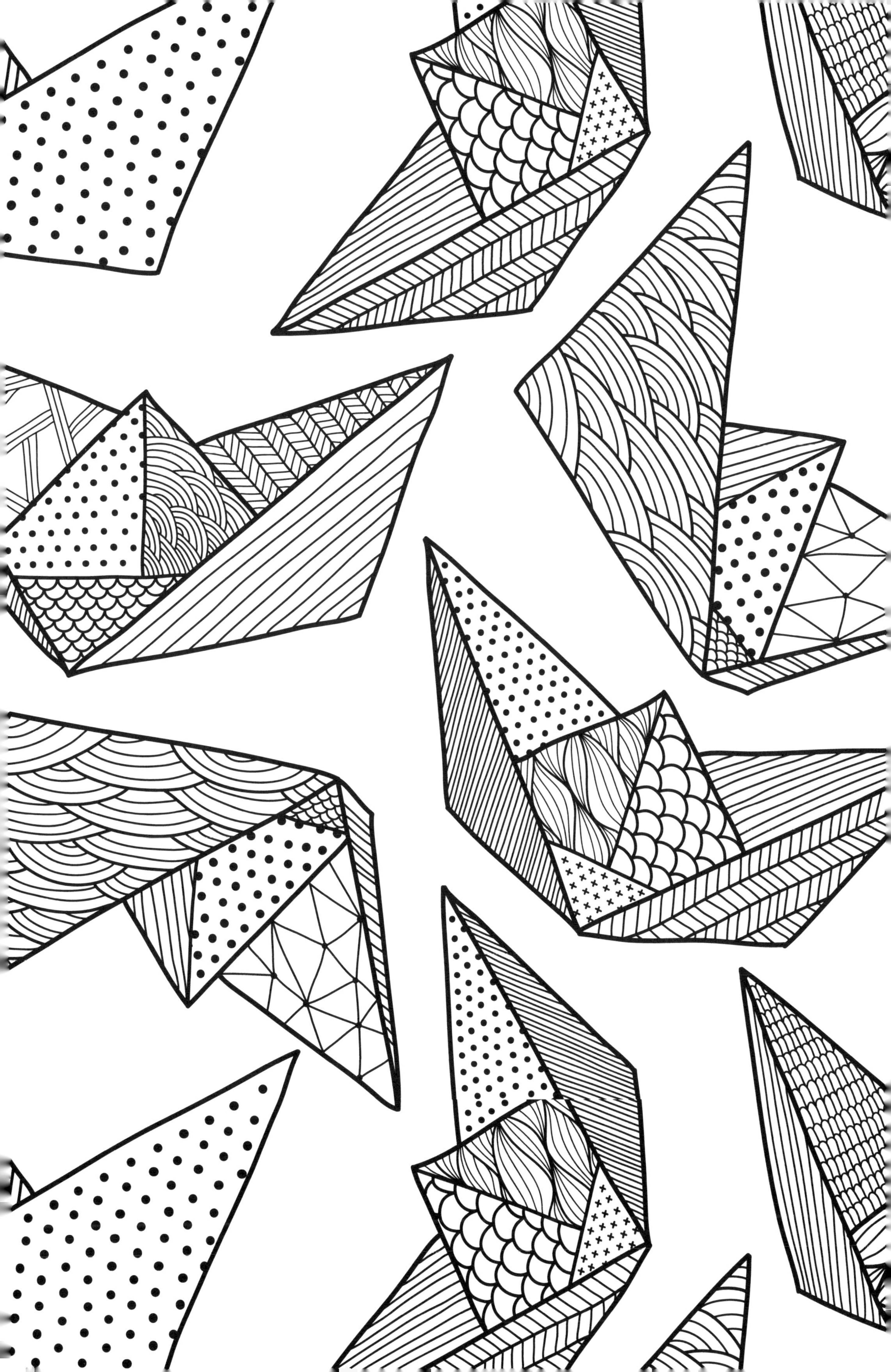

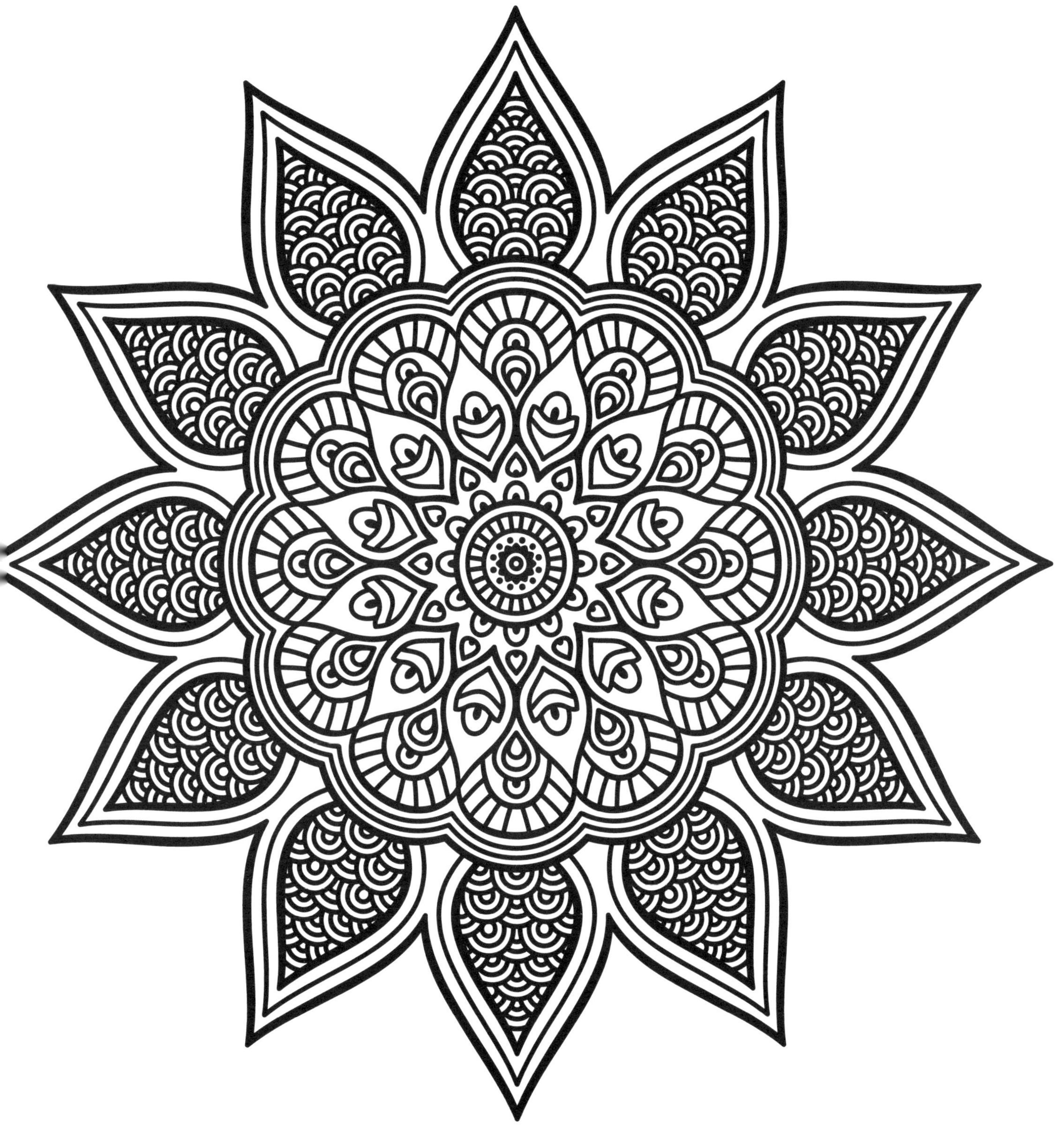

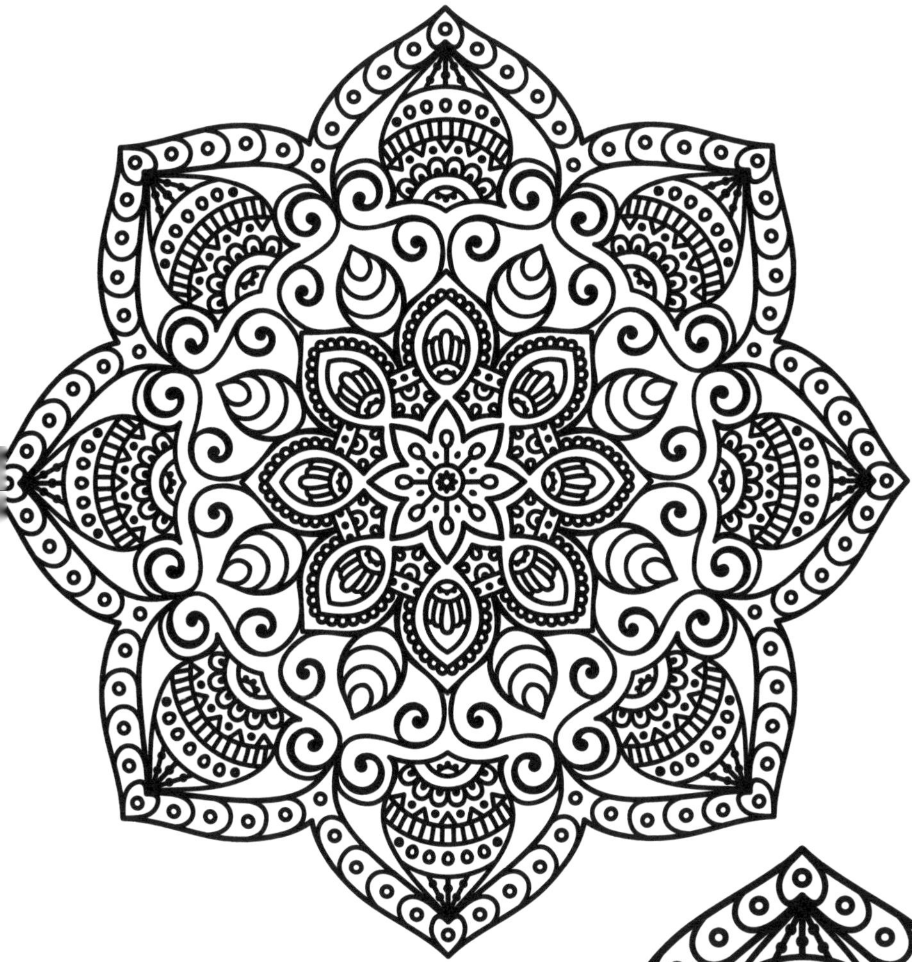
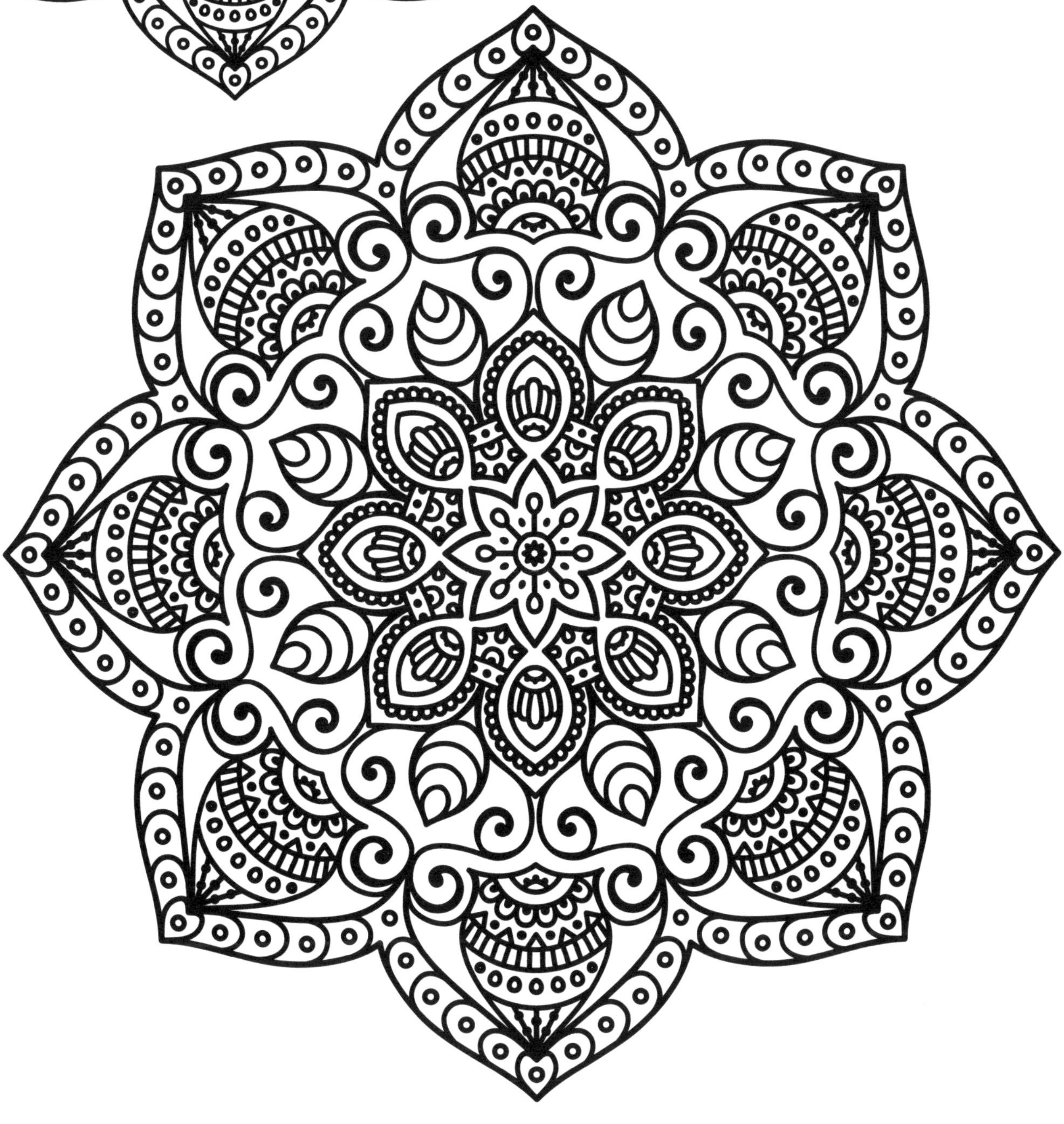

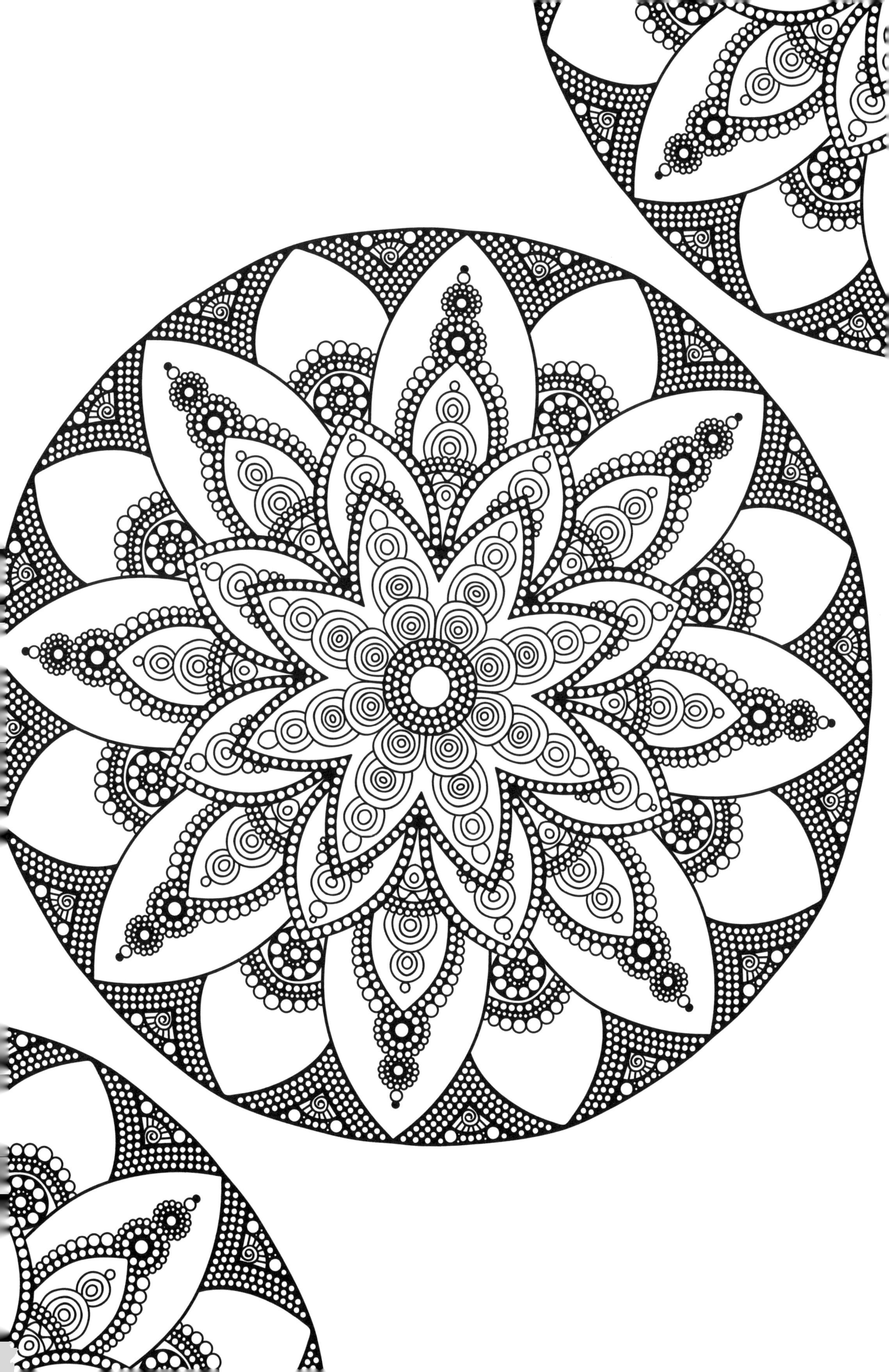

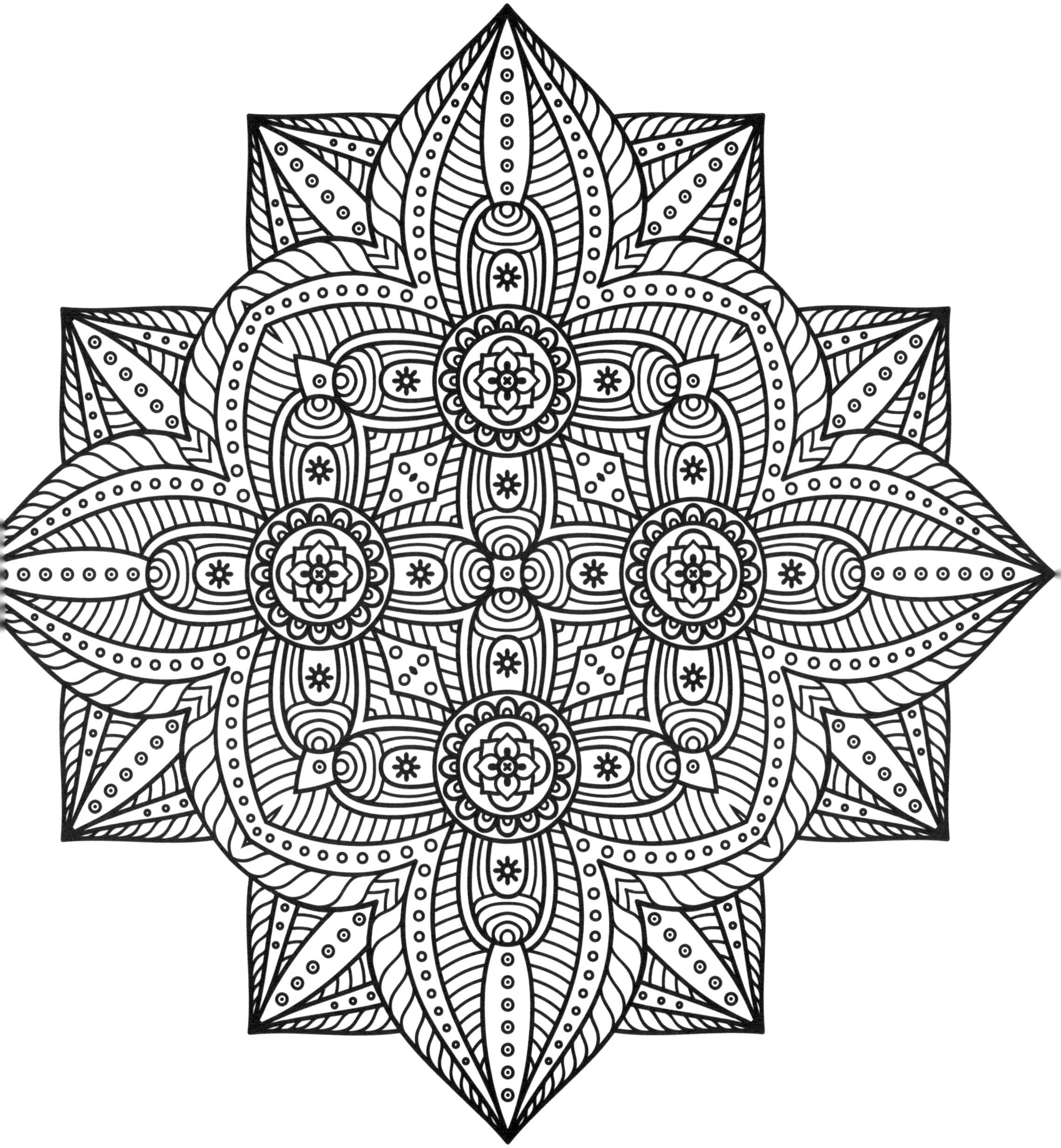

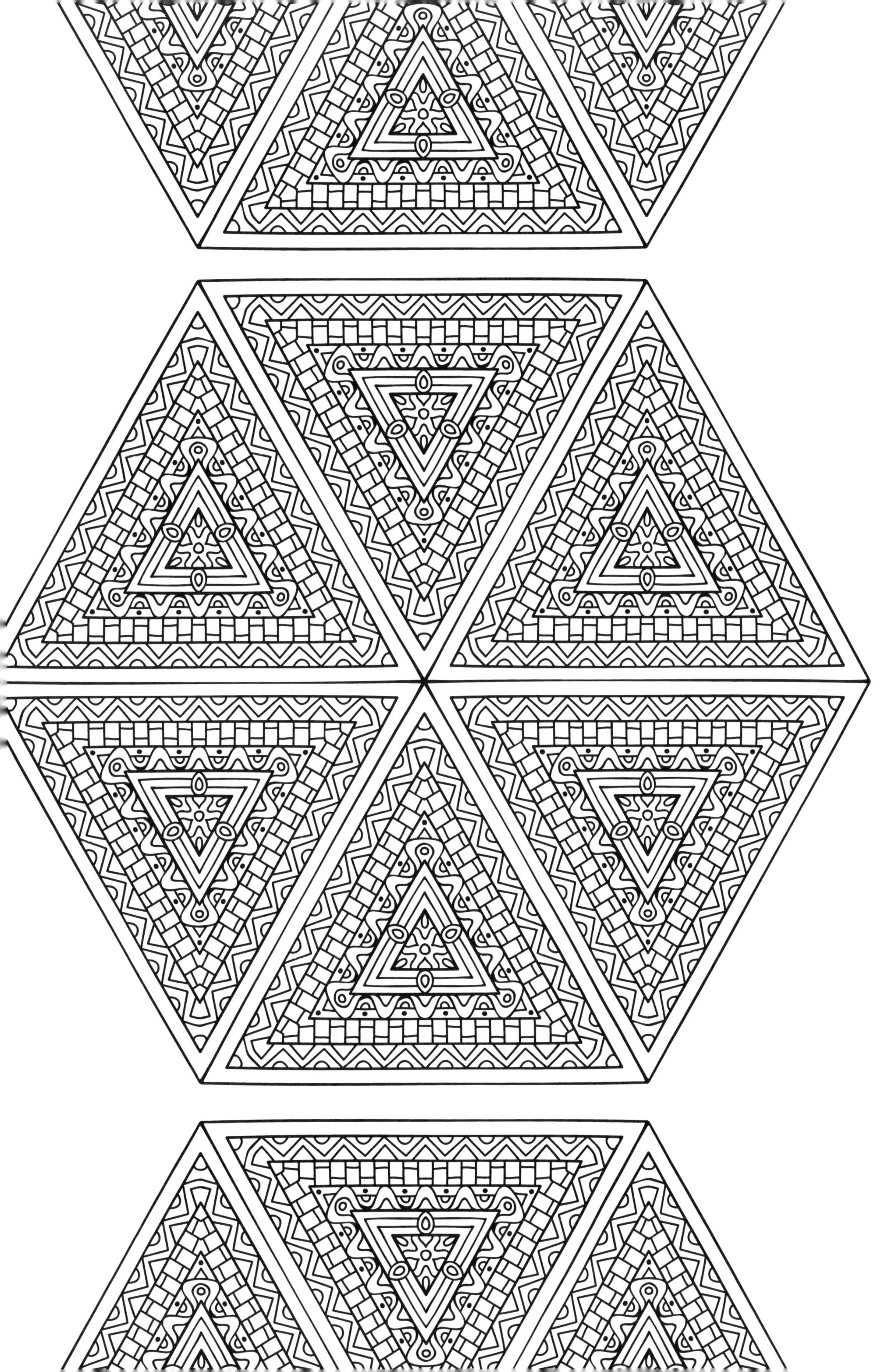

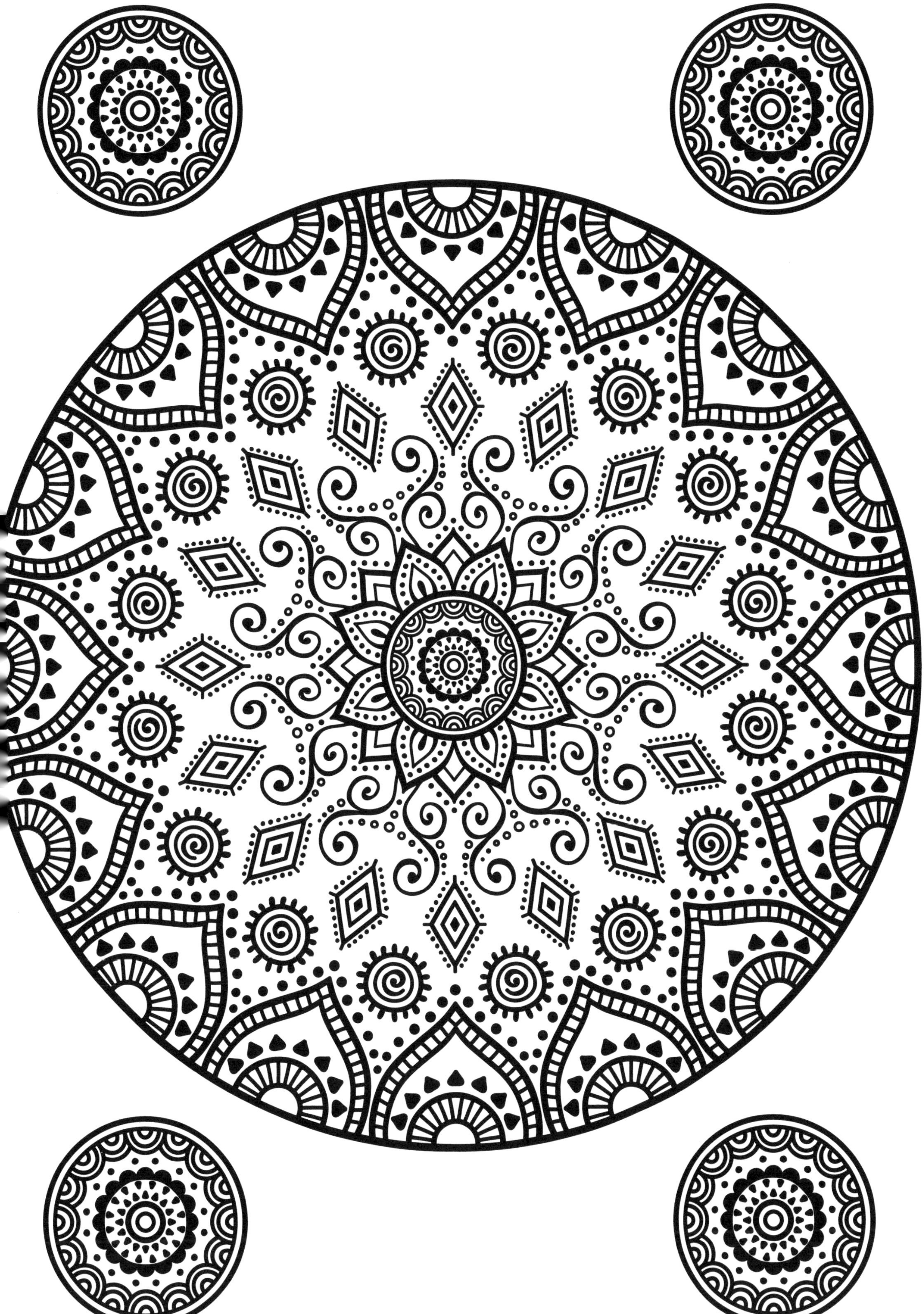

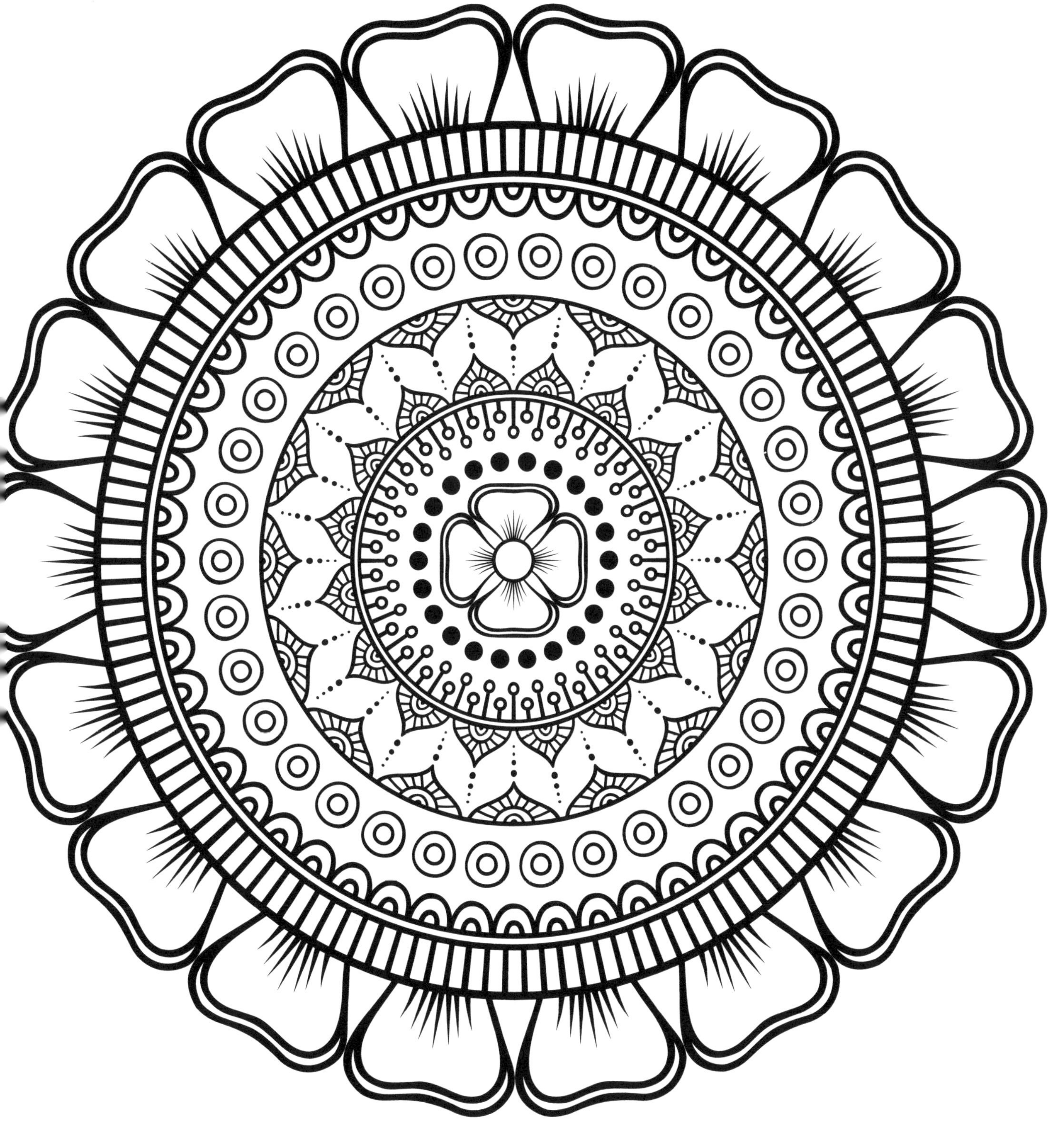

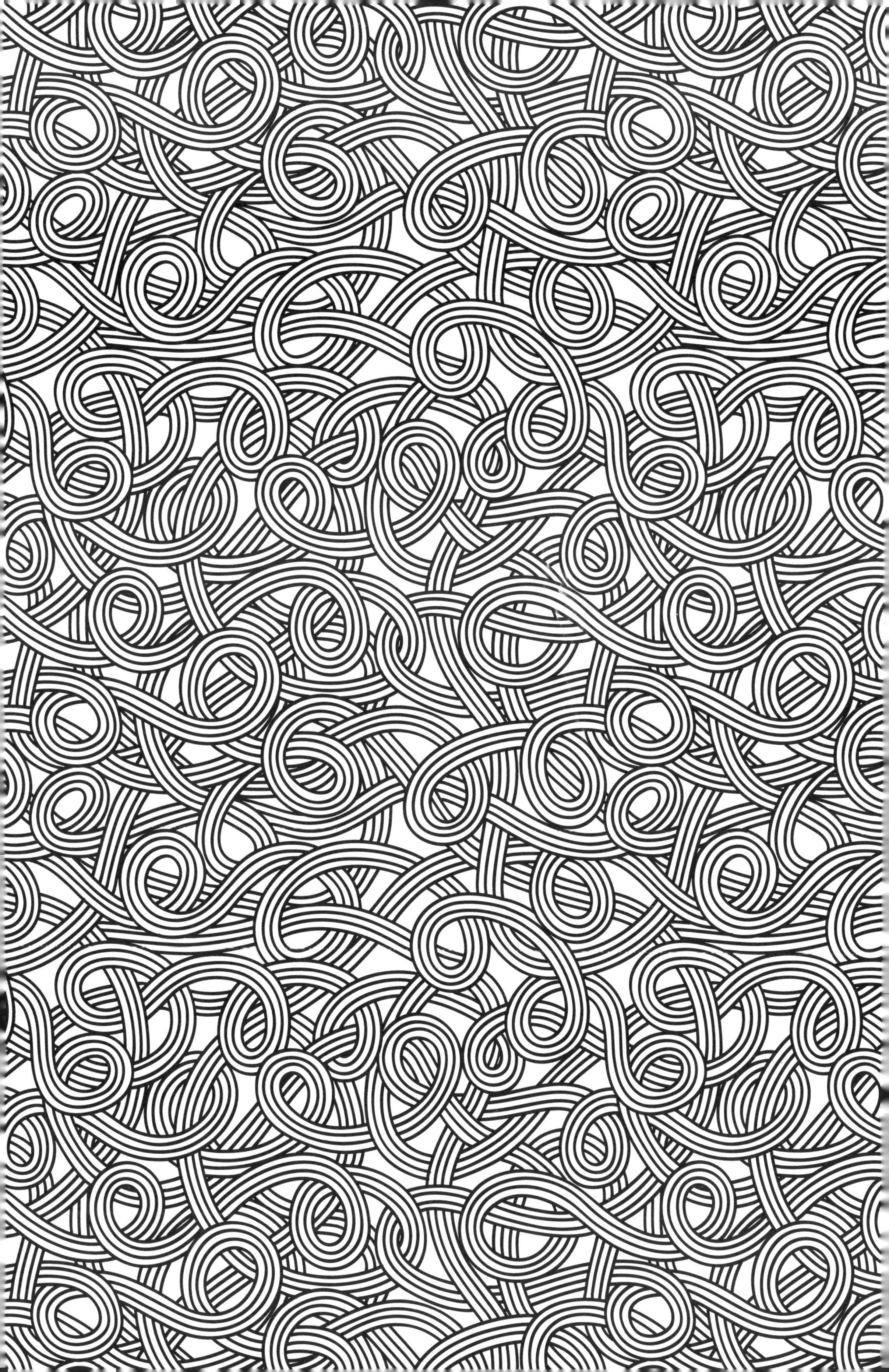

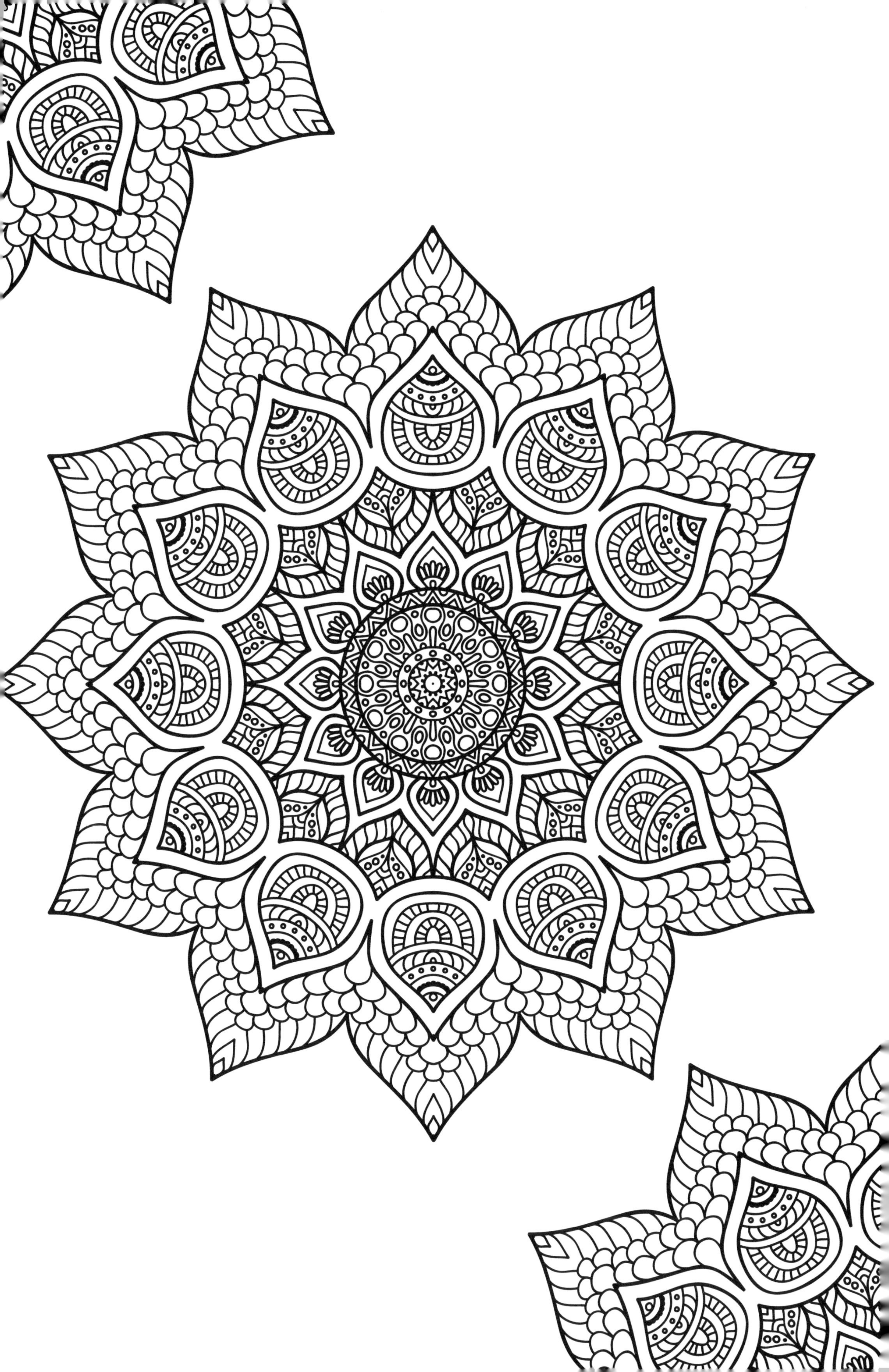

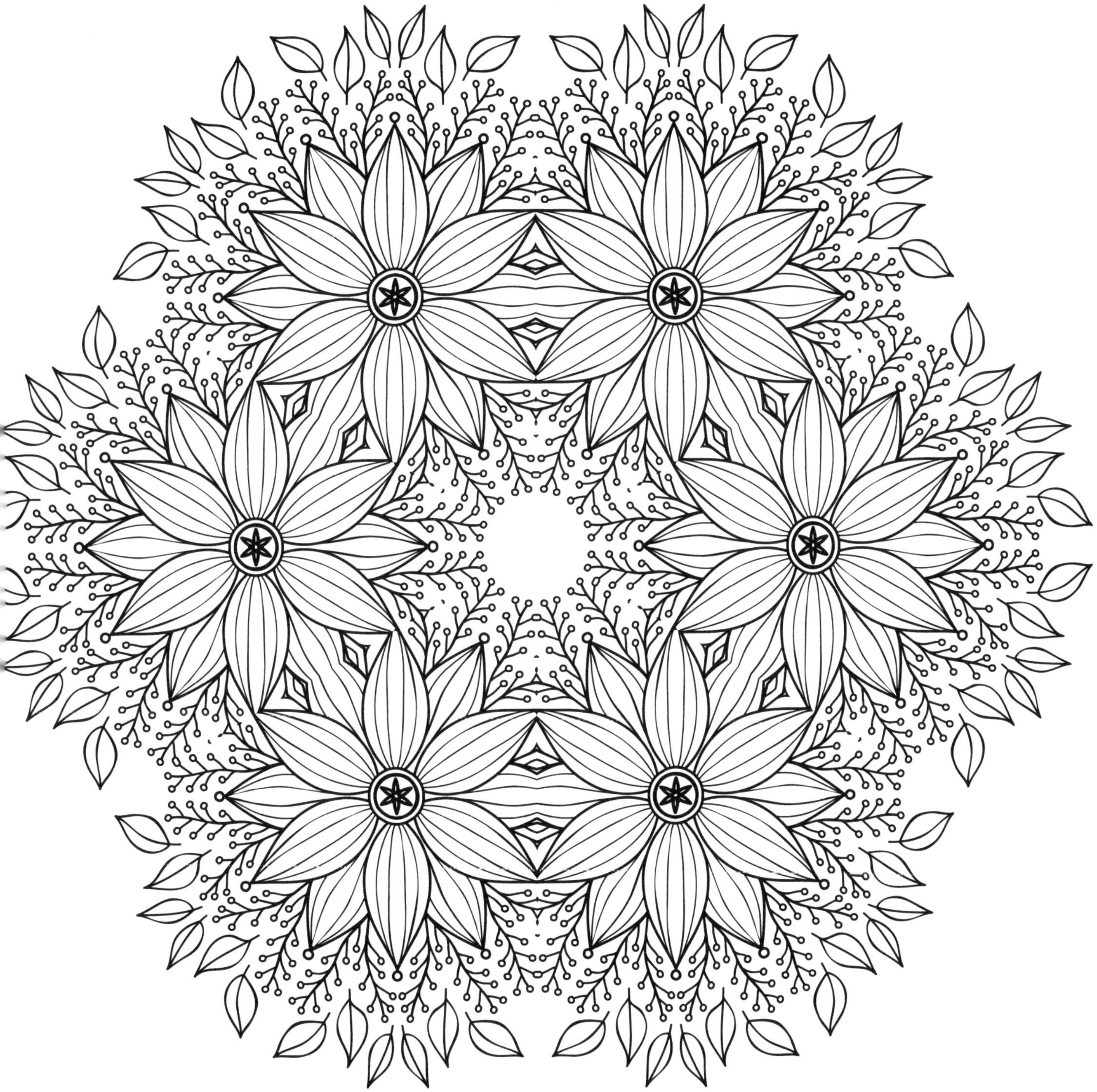

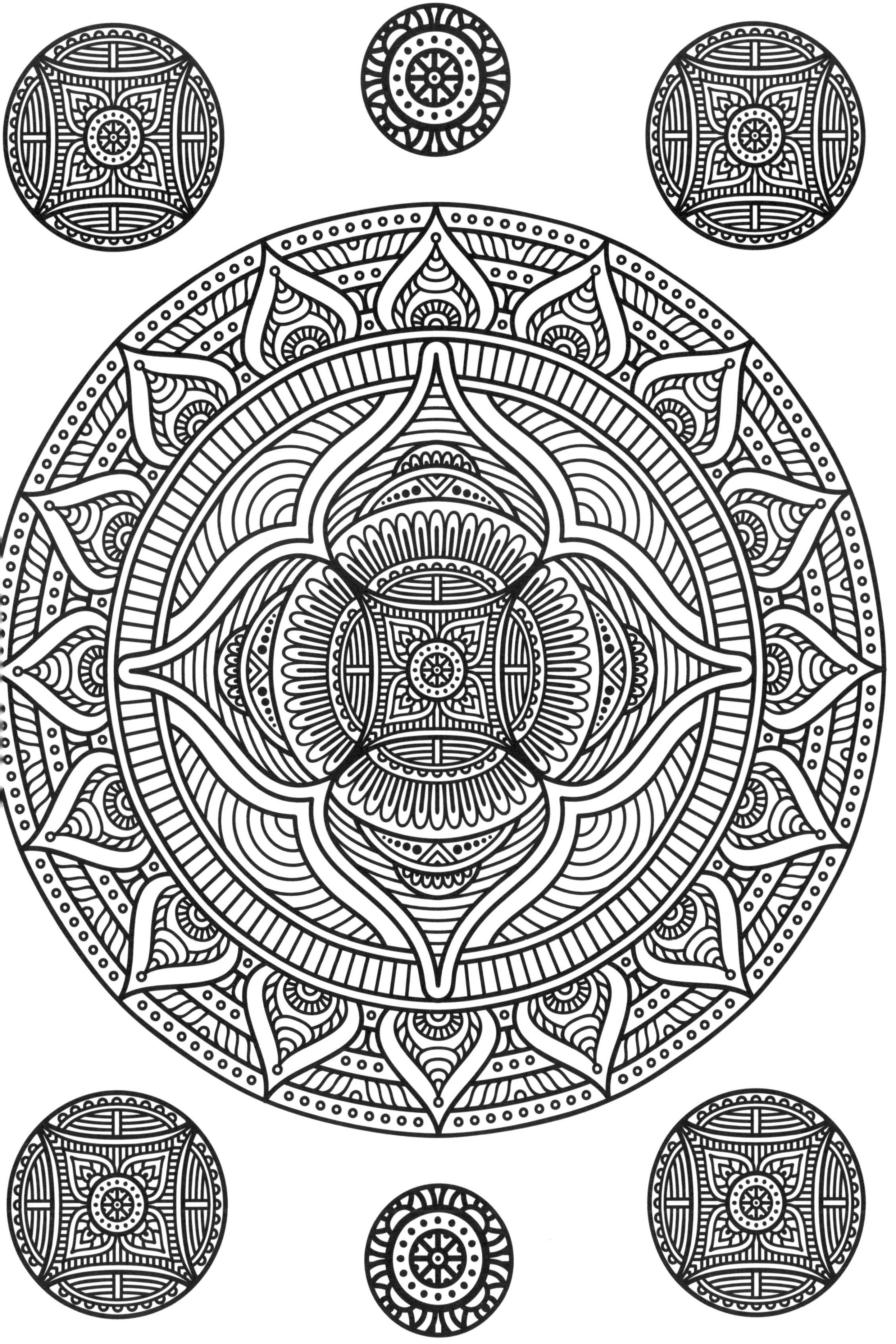

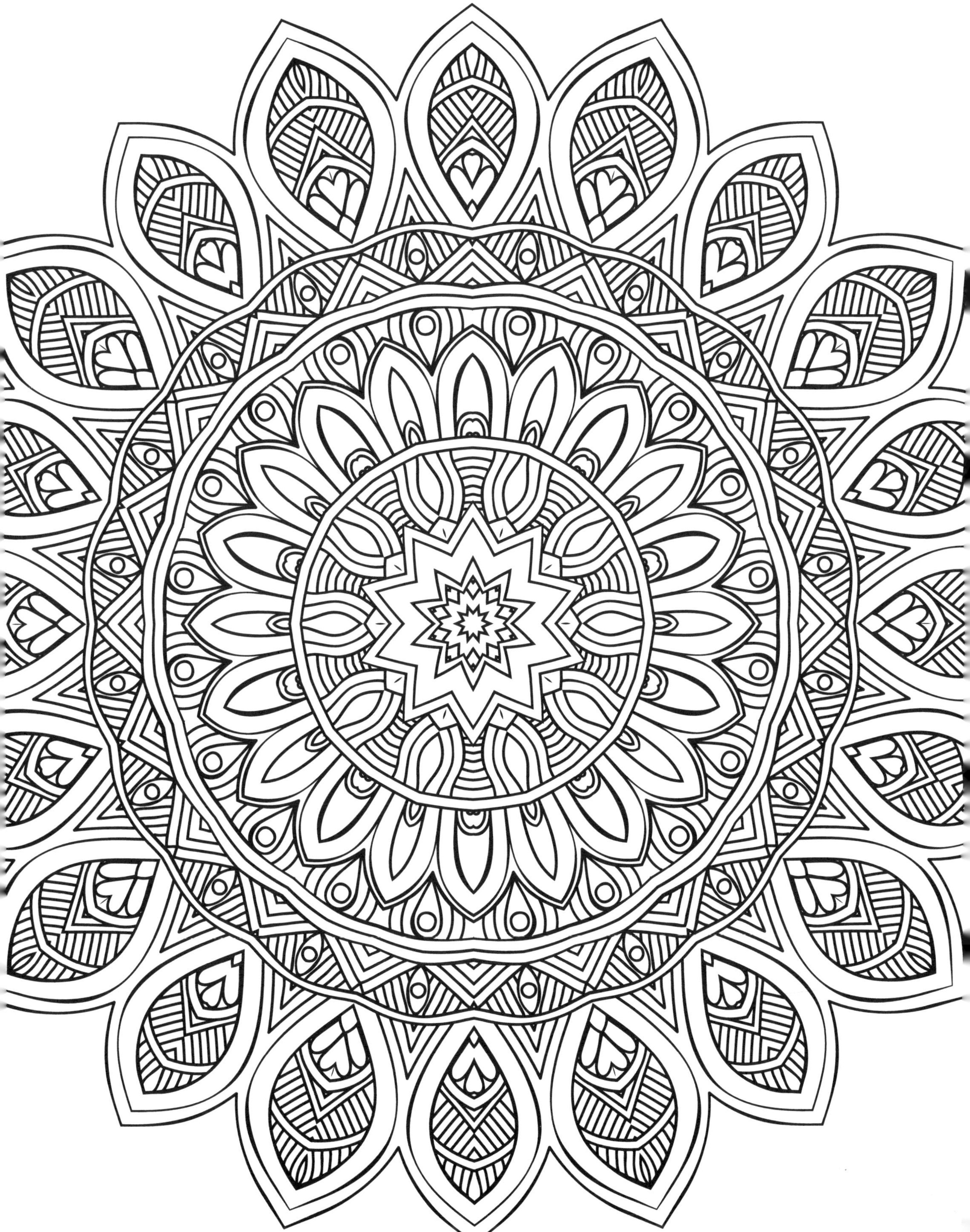

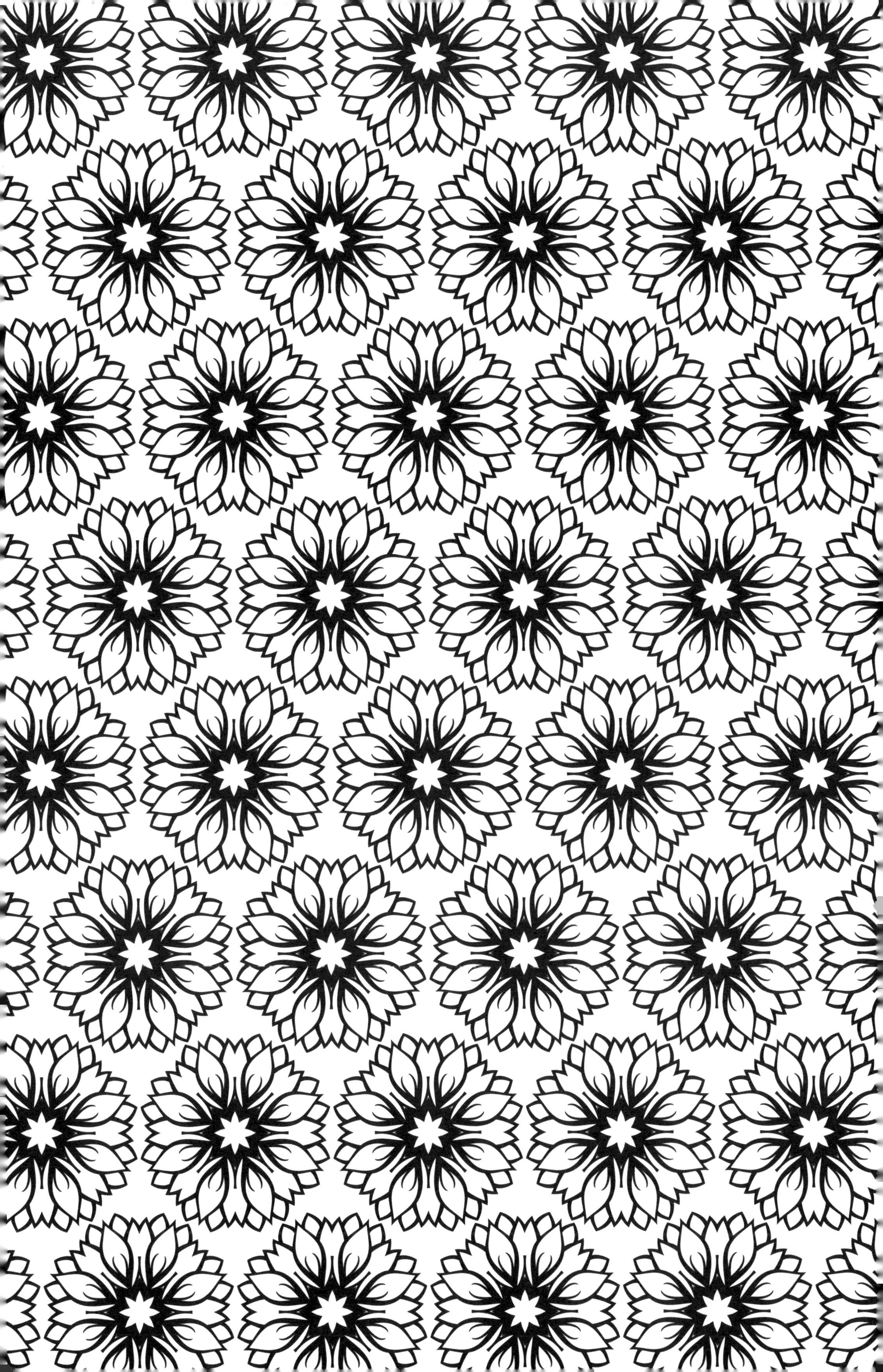

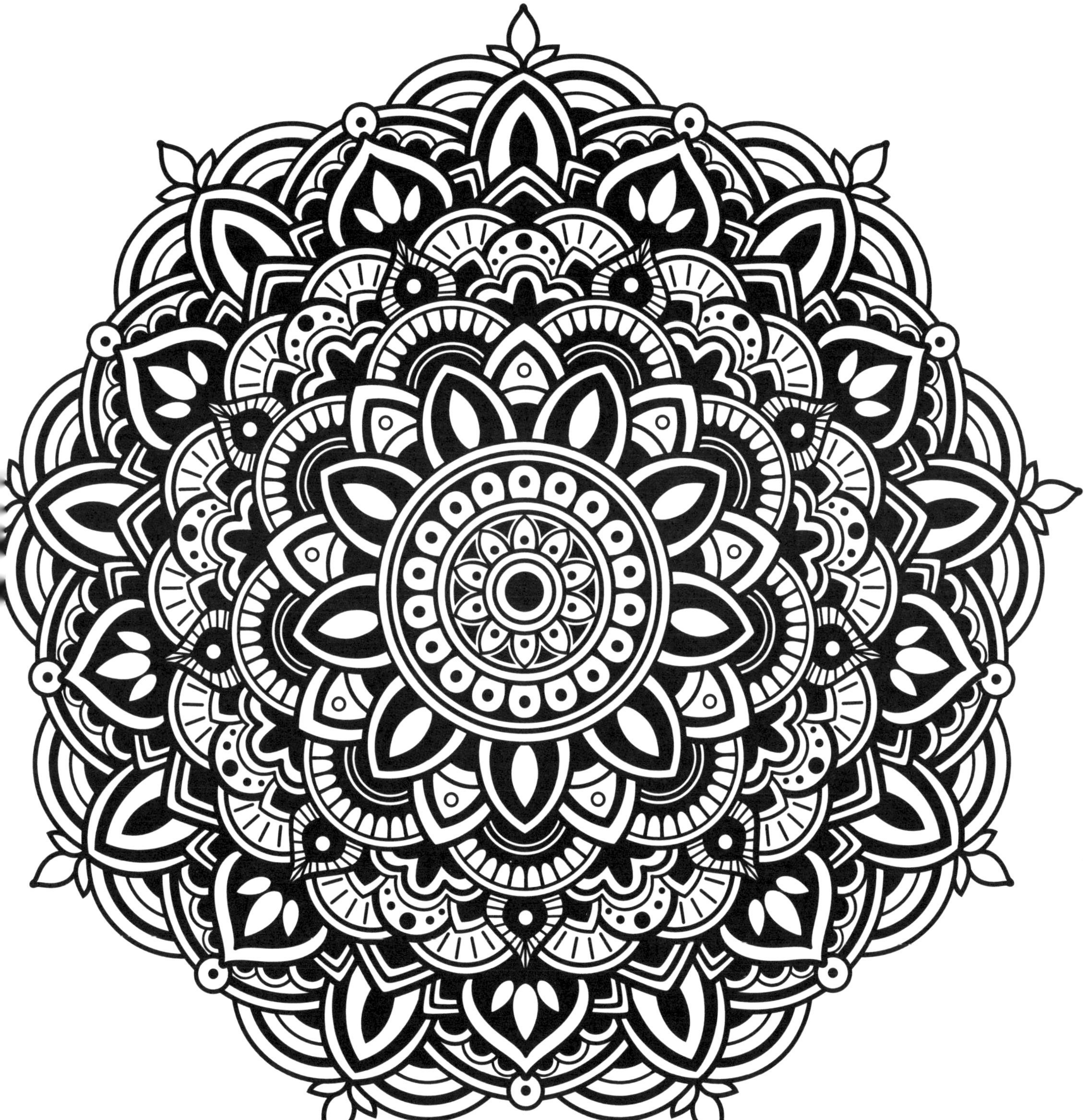

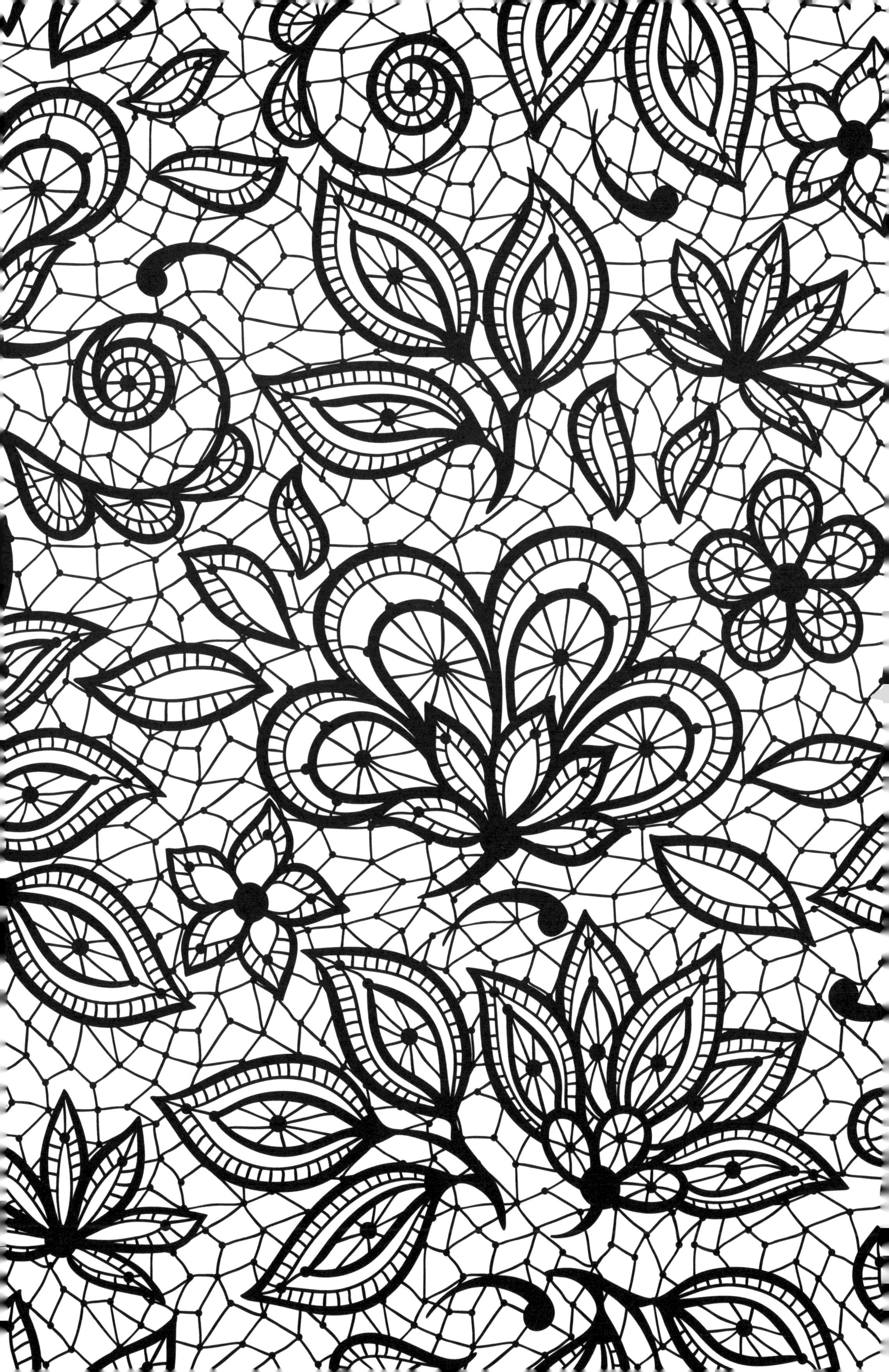

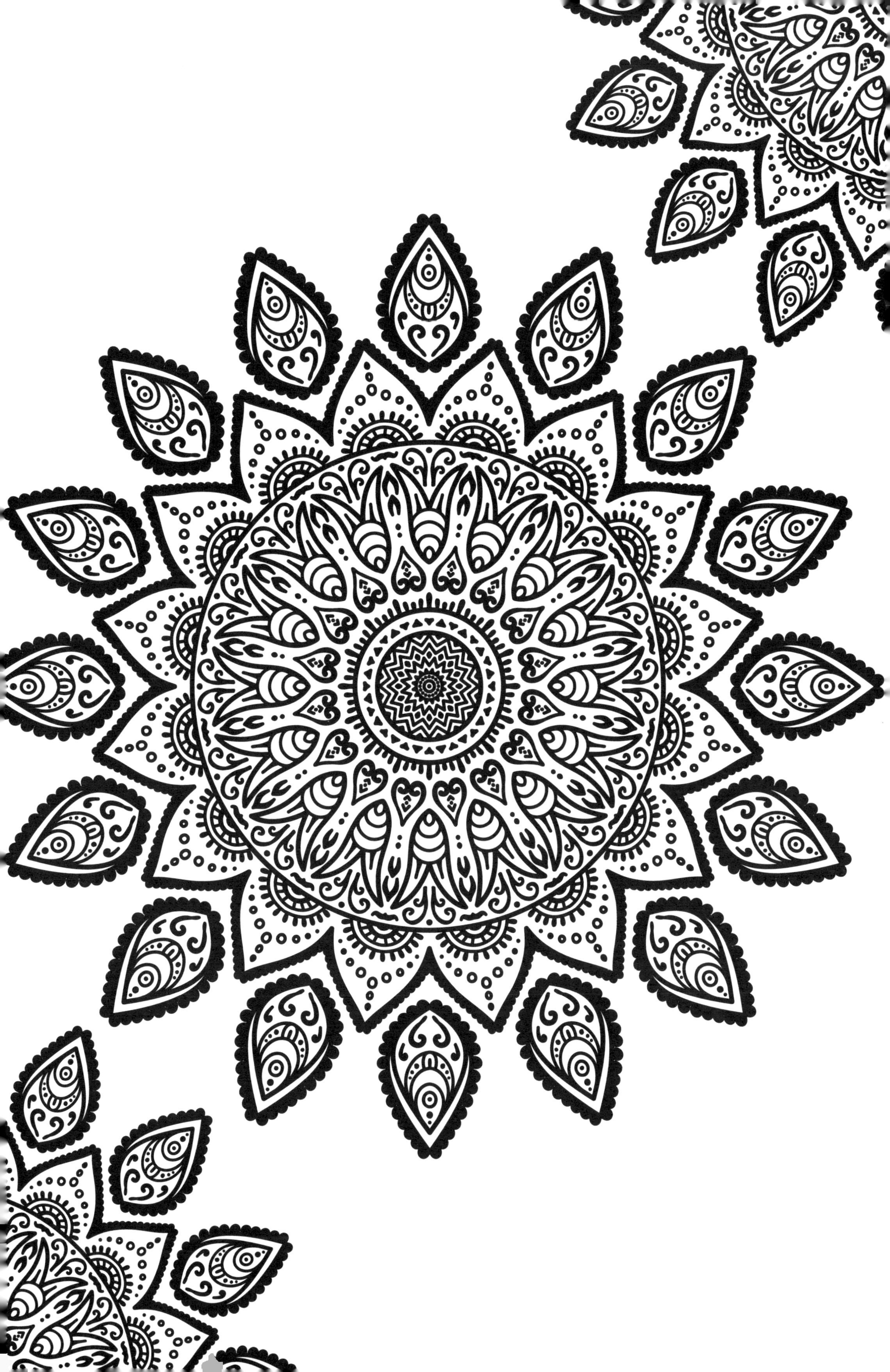

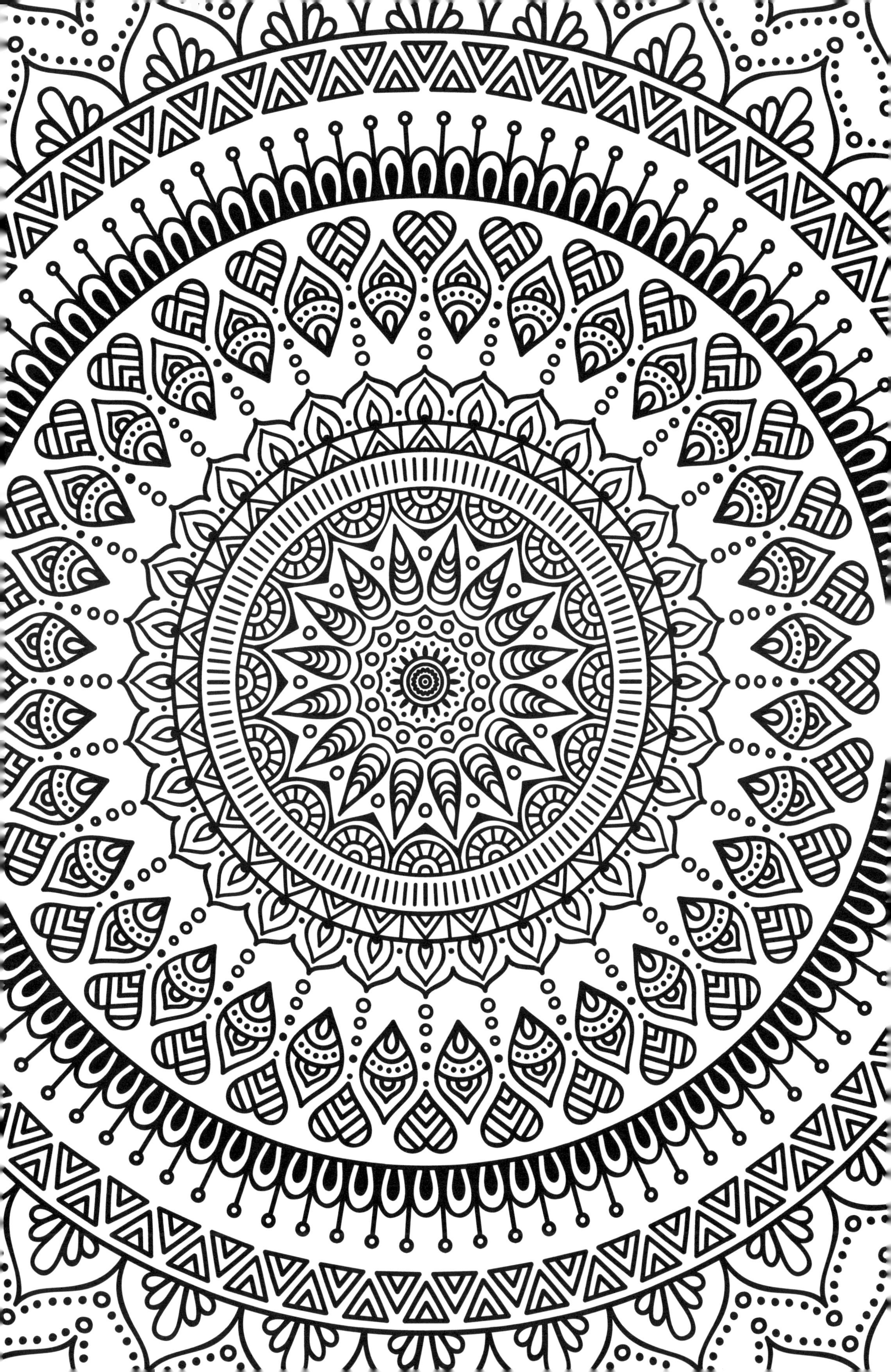